*As a child, I grew up with Denn[...]
him on an eldership team in a [...]
ited that same church, where Dennis now serves as senior pastor. As we
worshiped, I couldn't help but weep—because of the sense of sonship and
the Father's love that permeated the lives of those in that place. The examples and principles shared in this book are insightful and encouraging. But even greater, the changed and transformed lives in that community of believers give tangible and concrete evidence that those principles
can, in reality, rebuild broken lives—both spiritually and physically.
Thanks, Dennis, for sharing your life message with the rest of us!*
—Pastor Gil Miller, Desert Streams Church, Bend, Oregon

*A pre-adopt MUST. This book is comprehensive and straight forward
about God's redemptive purpose for each of us! For those who have already adopted, be encouraged and have hope! Dennis has turned over
many stones regarding the issue of adoption. There is too much wisdom
in Dennis' words to not consider reading this.*
—Chanda Bosanac, Operations Manager, *The Northwest Christian Community Foundation*

*Having been involved in helping people receive our heavenly Father's
love for over 15 years, I realize just how much understanding the spirit of
adoption is, in dealing with rejection. I do not know another pastor, mentor or friend like Dennis Nice who exemplifies the grace and mercy of
adoption and puts "feet to his faith" in his own choice to extend that love
to his adopted boys. This book is a must read for those who still struggle
with their own pain of being unloved and rejoice in OUR FATHER'S love
letter to us.*
—Rev. Peter J. DePaoli, Director, *Reclaiming Victory Ministries, Dis-
cipleship Training*

*This book is a "must read" for anyone who has adopted children. It is
also a "must read" for understanding what it means to be a "parent."
It's a "must read" as well, for Christians to understand the "spirit of
adoption!"*
—John David Hicks, *Evangelist and President of Faith Encounter, Inc.*

Exploring the Spirit of Adoption

Healing the Heart of the Fatherless

Dennis L. Nice

Partnership
Publications

A Division of House to House Publications

Disclaimer The statements contained in this book are expressions of my opinion based on personal parenting experience and the anecdotal evidence gathered from many other adoptive and foster parents, some who have been in my spiritual care. It is my personal belief that when counseling is required, whenever possible, one should seek professionals who have a Biblical foundation and basis for their worldview. He who has created us, knows us best and has revealed, through the scriptures, help in time of need. No part of this book should be construed as professional advice, nor should it be substituted for professional evaluation and subsequent care.

Partnership Publications
A Division of House to House Publications
www.H2HP.com

ISBN 978-0-9778614-3-9

Dedication

To Margaret:
*Woman of wisdom, the light of my life,
discerner of all things, good and evil.*

To Joshua and Daniel:
My sons with whom there has been a balance of trade.

To Angie, Christie and Debbie:
You have opened your hearts and homes to your brothers.

Acknowledgments

I am grateful for the encouragement and prodding of my friend Fawna Heath who challenged me in various ways, including purchasing advance copies of the book, to finish this project. Her help and suggestions through editing have been invaluable to me on this maiden voyage called writing. She too, is an adoptive mother who shares my passion to get this story out.

The cover art of this book represents the melding of two divergent paths. Adopter and adoptee are brought together in the loving harmony of joined hearts, stitched together with the transforming thread of the Holy Spirit. My gratitude is extended to Reid Phillips for capturing my heart for adoption through his God-given creative talent.

Contents

Exploring the Spirit of Adoption

Foreword

This is a book that has been begging to be written and Dennis Nice is the person for the task. While some authors may decide to write a book on a given subject, this message has been birthed through Dennis' life and experiences. God has blessed Dennis with both the experience and understanding of adoption. He and his wife Margaret have opened their hearts and home to two wonderful young men who needed parents. God also knew that Dennis and Margaret needed Joshua and Daniel to complete their family. Dennis and Margaret have also been blessed with three biological daughters, one of whom, along with her husband, has presented them with adopted grandchildren. Dennis writes with gentle wisdom that deals concisely with issues at the heart of adoption in its broadest and most poignant aspects. He addresses the reader from the perspective of having "been there" but does not give the impression that he has arrived at final understanding.

We live in an age in which most cultures are experiencing an unsettling increase in the numbers of those who are fatherless. Some children experience the physical absence of a father for various reasons. Others have a paternal figure that does not provide a father's genuine love and care. God is prompting many, like some of you who read this book, to respond practically to the need for providing for the fatherless. If you have chosen to read this book as a resource to guide you through the initial phases of adoption of your child, you will not be disappointed.

You will gain much insight and be given practical advice for helping your child make the gigantic leap from his or her birth situation into your family. You will gain helpful wisdom to understand your own adjustments that must be addressed. However, there is much more in this book! As you read, your focus being on the adoptive process and its intricacies, you will find that Dennis has invited you to venture beyond your involvement with your own child and into a deeper relationship with your Heavenly Father who has wide-open arms for you. Your own success as an adoptive parent or as a citizen will be dependent to a large degree on your own abandonment to your Heavenly Father who has prepared His home for you.

Travel thoughtfully on this journey with Dennis as you assimilate what God will show you. My prayer for you at the end of the day is that you truly know Him who is the lover and keeper of your soul! Thanks, Dennis for urging us to truly belong.

Wayne Shenk, D.Min.
Vanderhoof, British Columbia, Canada

Introduction

For as many as are led by the Spirit of God, these are sons of God. For you did not receive the spirit of bondage again to fear, but you received the Spirit of adoption by whom we cry out, "Abba, Father." The Spirit Himself bears witness with our spirit that we are children of God (Romans 8:14-16).

I am a father and a grandfather, husband, brother and friend, but most importantly, I am a son of the Father. I have received the spiritual adoption of a Father who loves me and cares for me unconditionally.

I pastor a church upon which Father God has placed a *Spirit of adoption.* Our church fellowship has grown to include between thirty and forty adoptive and foster children in the last ten years. I have also served on the board of a Christian adoption agency for a number of years. Both of these responsibilities have afforded me wide exposure to both the difficulties and the joys of adoption, through the varied experiences our adoptive families have encountered.

After raising three biological daughters, my wife and I heard the call to open our hearts and home to the fatherless. We have two twelve year old sons who have come to us from the West African nation of Liberia. They were birthed and begun in the cauldron of African wartime, witness to every type of inhumanity that man can perpetrate. We have not arrived at the end of the road. Quite the contrary, sometimes it seems like we are just beginning...again and again.

Since I am neither theologian nor psychologist, in the pages that follow it is not my intention to do a theological treatise on what the Apostle Paul was referring to when he wrote the phrase,

Spirit of adoption, found in the opening verses. I do, however, hope to capture a glimpse of the revelation the Apostle Paul imparted, which is revealed through the use of that phrase.

My purpose is not to convince you to adopt, although I would recommend it heartily. I hope to reveal some of the emotional mechanisms at work—not only for the adoptive child, but for every child of God who has not yet embraced the Spirit of adoption. Indeed, the mechanisms in play are not unique to adoptive or foster children, just exaggerated in these situations. Issues of abandonment and rejection are common to all who have grown up in less than nurturing environments. If you find yourself in this place, I believe the Father in heaven will guide you on your journey to wholeness.

I hope to share some revelation, bring some encouragement and possibly foster some understanding for two groups of people—those who find themselves in the throes of the adoptive or fostering process and those who need to know about and receive the Spiritual adoption of a Father who loves them with an everlasting and unconditional love.

Pure and undefiled religion before God and the Father is this: to visit orphans and widows in their trouble...(James 1:27a).

I asked the Lord one day, "Why is this pure and undefiled?" I felt He impressed on my heart the thought that this is one of the very few activities we can engage in that should have no expectation of return. We are simply called to love and to give. It pleases the Father because it is a manifestation of His adoptive heart of which we have all been the privileged recipient, if we know Him. What can the orphan or widow give in return? Indeed, what do any of us have to offer to God? Even our ability to love Him is dependent on the fact that He loved us first!

Chapter 1

The Father's View

It was a cool, somewhat foggy morning in the fall of 1988. I was driving our company van from one town to another to begin a new job. As I listened to the radio in a half-aware state, a question came unbidden to my mind, exploding into my consciousness. Now, I know this question may sound a bit morbid to you, but I was keenly aware that it was not one of my own design. "What would you want to say at Margaret's funeral?"

My wife wasn't dying! She wasn't even sick. The question was so odd that it commanded my complete attention. As I mulled it over, my thoughts ran freely over the previous fourteen years of marriage. Our marriage was strong and solid. We were very much in love and our children were leaving childhood and beginning the transition to adolescence.

Then the answer hit me!

The week I met Margaret in 1973, she knew our developing relationship was quite possibly becoming something different from what she had previously experienced. She felt it was necessary to share her personal story with me so there would be no surprises in our relationship. Prior to our meeting, as a young teenager, Margaret had become pregnant. As many were beginning to do in those days, the escape route of abortion was chosen as the alternative to the stigma of out of wedlock childbearing.

This choice has caused many to experience devastating emotional pain and suffering as they come to grips with issues that surround choosing to end the life of their unborn child. My response to the question that day in 1988, was cast in the light of Margaret's history of abortion, loss, grieving and healing.

Responding to that morning's initial question, I spoke out loud in the van, "I would want to say that while today is sad for us, it is the happiest day of Margaret's life as she is reunited with a son she never got to meet!" Suddenly, I was inundated with a mixture of grief and joy as tears began to flow at the thought of such an occasion. Immediately, the van I was driving became filled with the sense of an overwhelming presence of Jesus followed by what can only be described as a gripping and intense desire in my heart to adopt this child I had never known.

It was my first encounter with the beginnings of an understanding of what must be on the heart of heavenly Father as He looks at the brokenness of our lives.

I had never even considered the possibility of adoption. It wasn't something that had ever entered into my consciousness or realm of desire. In fact, it was an idea I was resistant to. We were happy with the size and composition of our family. Because of this, I began to have an emerging awareness that something of a supernatural character was taking place.

It was my first encounter with the beginnings of an understanding of what must be on the heart of heavenly Father as He

Exploring the Spirit of Adoption

looks at the brokenness of our lives. So many people think that relationship with God is defined by some legalistic list of rules. They believe He is an angry God just waiting to pounce on those who dare to take a misstep, incurring the wrath of the Almighty.

Quite the contrary! He is motivated by love and compassion for people who are caught in the ravages of sin. The intensity of His heart towards us is unfathomable as He longs to bring us, His wayward children, under the protective care of His adoptive heart through the Spirit of adoption. He loves us and lives to bring healing to the broken. He desires to bring family to those who are lonely and a peaceful port to the outcast, caught in the storms of life.

Steps to freedom

All these feelings and more enveloped me that day as God began laying new foundation stones of our future life together. Margaret and I were led through many subsequent steps of grieving and healing from that day forward as the Father lovingly guided us to emotional health and freedom.

That week, as we prayed together, we took responsibility for that unborn child. We named him, released him to the Father's care and began the process of receiving His love to fill the void of emptiness and loss.

Revelation 3:12 contains an interesting perspective of the Father's view:

He who overcomes, I will make him a pillar in the temple of My God, and he shall go out no more. I will write on him the name of My God and the name of the city of My God, the New Jerusalem, which comes down out of heaven from My God. And I will write on him My new name.

Everyone has available to them a new adoptive identity that is found in Father. No longer do you have to be named and identified by the circumstances of your past life. You can be known by a redeemed view that Father has in store for you. New life demands a new identity. He gives that identity as a token of His love.

Now, eighteen years later, the redemptive plan of God has come full circle in our lives. That which the enemy of our souls tried to steal from us has been redeemed and restored, many times over. It is not only through our biological and adoptive children and grandchildren, but Margaret now serves as the executive director of a Christian adoption agency, where she sees God's redeeming love replicated over and over as many children are united with their forever homes.

Chapter 2

Adoption—
A Thumbnail Sketch

"**D**ad, please pray!"

It was our oldest daughter, Angie, on the phone. Two years earlier, she, and her husband Steve, had experienced the loss of their daughter, little Olivia. Born prematurely at 25 weeks, she slipped away into eternity after only ten brief days with us. During the ensuing year, another daughter, Eliana Grace, was born, bringing joy to the house. It was then that Angie and Steve decided to pursue the idea of adoption. A benefactor stepped forward who offered to pay for their adoption costs, if they chose to follow through. They opted for a pair of three year olds from Liberia—a beautiful little girl and handsome boy they named Lillie and Nathaniel.

The urgent call was prompted by a typical African transportation emergency. The children were being escorted by a Liberian national who brought the children out of Liberia as far as Abidjan, Ivory Coast. The original flight for the traveling party had been canceled because of an airline bankruptcy. A hastily arranged flight out of Liberia and the purchase of another $4000 worth of tickets brought them to Abidjan.

When our Liberian friend and escort tried to board the Air France jet with the children, he was rejected because a person of his country of origin was not allowed to travel through Paris without a special visa in hand. Middle of the night calls and faxes to the French Embassy miraculously brought a special visa appointment. Finally, the children were on their way.

Anticipation of adoption

A child is on the way! You've decided to adopt! Excitement is in the air as you plan to enter the invigorating, yet challenging world of parenting a child birthed by another. In a potentially adoptive family where father and mother are present, the wife is most often the first to "know." Just as a natural pregnancy produces changes in her body, of which she is generally first to become aware, in her spirit there are the stirrings of potential parenthood, the beginnings of a "call."

Maybe the seed was planted by an adoption television program, a magazine article, or perhaps a friend who has opened their heart in this way. But, the seed finds a ready womb. It can happen fast....as in the natural realm. The husband, on the other hand, is not at all prepared for "the talk." You know, the blindsiding that comes when she snuggles up and in that sweet voice begins to croon, "You know honey, I was just thinking...." Before long, the seed takes root in the heart of the husband as well.

You are embarking on one of the most fulfilling, stretching, arduous and intriguing adventures known to man.

You are embarking on one of the most fulfilling, stretching, arduous and intriguing adventures known to man. You have embraced the choosing and raising of a child who has come into this world in less than favorable circumstances, giving that child a new lease on life and the potentials it can hold. But be assured, this is no summer camp experience. Once embraced, this is a journey for the long haul. This is for life. It is not just a commitment; it is the beginning of a covenant, a covenant of love.

There are decisions to be made. Do you adopt nationally or internationally, open or closed adoption, age and gender, transracial or not? What is the effect on birth order to bring a child into your existing family? All of these issues and many more, come into play as you contemplate one of the most life changing of experiences.

The waiting begins

The emotional pregnancy can seem to be without end. There is a flurry of excitement and activity at the outset: application made to an agency, fingerprinting, background checks, pre-adopt classes, home study visits, then nothing for a long time; seemingly forever, especially if adopting internationally. Unstable governments, lost paperwork and INS (Immigration and Naturalization Service, now known as CIS) hoops to jump through, all add to the unpredictability of the "length of gestation." At least with a natural pregnancy you know that somewhere around nine months, something is bound to happen. In the case of an unwed mother giving up her child to you for adoption, waiting for the birth of your promised child can also be an excruciatingly unsettling process. Will she follow through as promised or change her mind at the last minute?

There are many types of adoptions however, and each is fraught with unanticipated complexities that can cause untold frustration. Some have waited years to see their dreams fulfilled.

It is at this time that deep frustration can set in for the waiting parents. You are sure the adoption agency or some government bureaucrat has intentionally set your file aside just because they really don't care. This is after all, "your child." Why aren't they doing everything in their power to move heaven and earth on your behalf? You are convinced that incompetence and laziness has taken over the powers that be.

There comes a time in this process where your adoption is completely and totally in the hands of unseen forces, and you are convinced that they have singled you out for cruel and unusual delay. The wait is killing you. I know what you're thinking: "If only we could just get our child home, then everything would just settle down and be okay."

Is that so?

The beginning stage

Actually, when your bundle of joy arrives, the honeymoon begins. There is the joy of discovery that comes with the new arrival and, depending on the age of your child and the experiences he or she has encountered, that initial flush of joy could last from two days to two years.

Just as with natural childbirth however, there will come a time when the new addition may begin to keep you up at night, attempting to piece together the emotional jigsaw puzzle this child embodies. Even a baby adopted from birth, has already had experiences, if only in the womb, that you will never be privy to. They have already been influenced by nature and nurture, many times in unknown ways. This is, after all, a real human being with relationships and experiences that will always predate yours.

In the adoption world, a child, by the age of three, is considered an "older child." Because the personality and basic characteristics of a child are formed by the age of six, most adoptive children have a well-formed history by the time they reach their "forever home." A three year old has already formed language skills and received all the resident information that has been communicated culturally in that process. Obviously, the older the child, the more history there is to work through.

The challenges of new spiritual birth

The same is true when we welcome the life changing presence of Jesus into our lives, though we are really more like the older child than the baby. We have been birthed and raised under the ownership of our fallen nature. Born in Adam's sin, we were steeped in a desire to please ourselves. The longer we have walked in "the world" the more baggage we carry. This is our history that contains all the hurt, wounding and brokenness we have experienced.

All the things we believe about ourselves and our relationships to others are shaped by our history and to what extent we have, or have not, received healing.

We have been trained by our experiences, programmed by our environments and have learned that others can't be trusted. "If you want something done right, you have to do it yourself." "All men are pigs!" "All women nag!" "Every time I get close to someone, they just hurt me!" You get the picture. All the things we believe about ourselves and our relationships to others are shaped by our history and to what extent we have, or have not, received healing. As it is with adoptive children, so it is with the Father's adoptive children. The forming of a new bond with our heavenly Father, believing in our hearts that He can be trusted, is a necessary part of our coming to wholeness.

Let the bonding begin!

Chapter 3

A Brief History of Adoption

A quick glance at past cultures reveals a long history of adoption, though not always in the form we experience it today. Hammurabi of Mesopotamia, circa 1750 B.C., had an extensive set of laws which governed adoption. The Code of Hammurabi, paragraphs 185-193 formed foundational understandings that led to modern day adoption.

In this code there are also some interesting twists that are somewhat curious. For example, once adopted and reared, a child could not return to his original father's house. However, if an artisan took in a child and taught the child his craft in an adoption/apprentice relationship, the child could not return to his original family, but if the artisan failed to teach the child a craft, then that child was free to return.

The few cultures of the ancient world that practiced adoption did so almost exclusively through adult adoption for the purpose of inheritance. The practice of adopting children was rare. In many cultures, if a man died without an heir, his estate became the property of the government much like we experience today. Adults were adopted into the family in order to pass on the family's wealth and traditions.

In biblical history, there is no record of adoption being legally integrated into the Old Testament Jewish law, even though Moses himself was adopted by Pharaoh's daughter as a baby. Samuel was also taken to the temple to be mentored and raised by Eli the priest. This seemed to be by simple agreement rather than by any established legality.

Certain African cultures still practice this relaxed approach today. In the culture of my African sons, if a father dies, his children are passed on to the oldest remaining brother in the family. Their mother is sent back to her family without her children. The primary purpose for this is to assure the children are raised in the bloodline of the father.

Foundations of modern adoptions

Contained within the body of Roman law is an article entitled, "Adoption." The Romans had perhaps the most extensive set of rules and laws regarding the process of adoption on record. The Roman Emperor, Justinian, issued a civil code called, "The Institutes" which contains adoption law. Again, in the Roman culture this was primarily, but not exclusively, adult adoption. It is precisely into this culture that the Apostle Paul wrote these words from Romans, chapter 8, verse 15:

> *For you did not receive the spirit of bondage again to fear, but you received the Spirit of adoption by whom we cry out, "Abba, Father."*

Paul was well aware of the culture into which he spoke these words. They were loaded with meaning for his intended audience. As I read the articles of Roman adoption law, I found they reveal some of the thinking which surrounded the Roman understanding of the process. This also gives some insight into the depth of truth Paul is communicating to us regarding our relationship to God.

First, the adoptee loses, or is cut off, from all legal rights to the old family, but gains all the equivalent rights in the new family. Second, the adoptee becomes the legal heir (or joint-heir) to the wealth of the estate of the new father. And finally, the old life was completely wiped out in the sense that all debts, both financial and legal were canceled. Apparently, no legal charges were to follow him into his new identity.

Biblical adoption defined

In the original Greek language of the New Testament, the word Paul uses for adoption is "huiothesia" which means "to place as a son." In certain Middle Eastern cultures there were even ceremonies by which a father could adopt his own son! A process was followed where a child would be placed in the care of a trusted slave or family servant as a tutor/mentor for the purpose of raising and educating him. He would then be called out of childhood into the realm of adulthood, presented to the father as ready for responsibility.

Ralph Mahoney of World Missionary Assistance Plan (World MAP) once wrote an article entitled, *Adoption*, in which he shared insight about this concept. He explained that at the appropriate age, generally as the child was nearing adulthood, a ceremony to receive a child into "sonship" could be celebrated. This officially conferred on the son the blessing of all family privileges with access to the family resources. He was a child by birth, but became a son by choice.

Cultural parallels

Many cultures practice various forms of this rite of passage. Young men or young women are set apart for training in the tenets of their specific culture as they pass through the process of coming of age. I have observed this in Africa where young people are separated from their families, their bodies painted in vivid colors to signal to others that they have entered this phase of life. A mentor is assigned to them to teach and train them in the ways of the tribe. After the appropriate length of time, they rejoin the others, received as adults to take their place as a productive member of the tribe.

Paul alludes to this process in Galatians 4:1-2:

Now I say that the heir, as long as he is a child, does not differ at all from a slave, though he is master of all, but is under guardians and stewards until the time appointed by the father.

Even Jesus, at His baptism by John, received the "calling out" of a son when a voice from heaven declared, "This is my beloved Son in whom I am well pleased. Hear Him!" Not only did the Father recognize Jesus as His son, He also declared the authority that was passed to Him.

This background information is important because Paul is showing a parallel here between adoption and our relationship to God. In our experiences with adoption, we have come to understand a simple, yet profound, truth. There is a difference between being born and being adopted! Every child who has been adopted first had to be born, but they are two entirely separate events.

> Even Jesus, at His baptism by John, received the "calling out" of a son when a voice from heaven declared, "This is My beloved Son in whom I am well pleased. Hear Him!"

First, our sons were born in Africa. Then, when our sons came to our home and we adopted them, they were "born again" into our family. I considered them my sons from that day forward. This is the Father's perspective towards us. From the time we ask Jesus to come into our life and save us from our sin by His shed blood, Father sees us as His children, "born again" into His family.

Receiving the Spirit of adoption

For adoptive children, however, it usually takes a significant period of time before they "receive" the Spirit of adoption. Even though my sons have been "born again" into my family, they are still in the process of being convinced in their emotional being that they can trust they are in a family who will love and care for them unconditionally. All of their past experiences create an emotional battle within them that rages on and on until they come to the place that they can receive their father's (and mother's) love!

The *decision* of adoption is quite different from the *process* of adoption. A child who is being adopted, in most cases, has no initial choice in the matter as a result of age. However, there comes a time in the life of every adoptee when they must, in return, give emotional agreement or ascent to the adoption. It sometimes happens early on, but usually takes a significant amount of time. There are also times when the child may appear accepting of their new life, then relapse into acting out old patterns of aggressive or passive-aggressive behavior, triggered by some new experience that is a reminder of rejection in their past.

As a pastor, many people I meet with, adopted or not, find themselves spiritually in this place. Because of the blows life has dealt them, their ability to trust a loving Father has been decimated and the ability to walk in spiritual and emotional victory just seems to elude them. They experience failure after failure until they finally want to give up. Even though they know

Jesus as Savior, they have not yet *received* the Father's adoption. Or, put another way, they have not yet received the "Spirit of adoption."

Receive the Father's love

Many have not come to terms with receiving a Father who loves them with an everlasting love. After all, their earthly experiences with father figures have left them broken and wanting. Perhaps, performance demanding fathers have clouded and skewed their understanding of what is to be truly received. They believe they are received based on performance and cannot comprehend being received and loved, based solely on who they are, a person of worth and value; based on who Father created them to be!

As stated earlier, in the Roman understanding of adoption, the adoptee must give up all rights to the old family. This must not be confused with forgetting where they came from. Quite the contrary! The path to healthy transition is paved with an understanding of one's own history, as far as it can be established. Almost every child has within, the desire to know where they have come from and they need to be told. There must, however, be transference of the bond, as well as a development of interdependence with the new family.

> Accepting or receiving the Spirit of adoption means the giving up of the emotional bond, the attachment to the life of the former family in order to bond with the new.

Accepting or receiving the Spirit of adoption means the giving up of the emotional bond, the attachment to the life of the former family in order to bond with the new. This is true for both the child and the family. If the family hangs on to the former family structure and does not flexibly make way for the new addition, failure to bond can be the inevitable end, ultimately leading to disruption of the adoption.

Older adoptive children tend to fantasize about the way it might have, or could have been. There might be a desire to return to the former state of being, no matter how unfulfilling, undesirable or dangerous it might have been. It is a phase almost every adoptee goes through and until they do, they have not completely received the Spirit of adoption. They must be patiently loved through these turbulent times.

Going back to "Egypt"

This tends to be the case spiritually as well. When the Israelites left the bondage of Egypt for the unpredictable journey of the desert, they soon began to grumble and complain to Moses for bringing them out into the desert to die because of the lack of food and water. In their whining and murmuring, they asked to be taken back to the predictable security of Egypt, even though it meant a return to slavery. Believers in Jesus who always have a hankering to go back to "Egypt" and feed at the trough of worldly pollution, are those who have not truly "tasted and seen that the Lord is good" (Psalm. 34:8). They have not yet received the Spirit of adoption. Jesus once said, *"You did not choose me, but I chose you..." (John. 15:16).* All of us need to come to terms with the fact that we have been chosen by God. For the adoptee, it is doubly important.

I heard the following story from an adoptive parent. Their adopted son, "Tommy," went to school for the first time in the first grade. After a few days, he came home crying and didn't want to return. Upon investigation, the mother discovered he had been teased repeatedly about being adopted. His mother, in righteous (I think) anger, sent Tommy back to school and told him that if it happened again, he was to tell them, "Your parents had to keep you, my parents *chose* me!"

You have been chosen!

As children of the heavenly Father, we also have been chosen! We must embrace the fact that we have been transferred from the kingdom of darkness, from the fallen family of this world, into the heavenly family, the kingdom of light. Chosen! Think of it! The longer we pine for the past (the leeks, garlic and onions of Egypt) the longer we will be prevented from partaking of the milk and honey in the promised land of our inheritance! The old life has been wiped out! All debts have been canceled!

I have heard it taught that under Roman law, even if the person had committed murder in the old life, after the adoption, all charges and resulting punishment were dropped. The former person was considered to no longer exist. We can be free from the sins of generations past! As adoptees of the heavenly Father, we can be free from those sins and habits which have for so long, controlled and exercised dominion over us. We can walk in the assurance that as sons and daughters of the Father, we are accepted, loved and valued by Him!

> Too often the church has not exhibited the flexibility needed, to welcome into the family the wounded we encounter.

Barriers to integration

Too often the church has not exhibited the flexibility needed, to welcome into the family the wounded we encounter. If the church, like the adoptive family, is not willing to embrace and openly receive the new addition to the spiritual family, then the requisite bonding will not occur. The church must shoulder the greater weight in being gracious, loving, patient and receiving, as the "birth order" is being adjusted.

I was once a part of a church that experienced a great influx of new believers and members. Those who had been with the church for many years were soon outnumbered by the new growth. Soon, accusations of, "they're taking our church away from us" began to surface. Things had changed! New members had invaded the "birth order." The desire to remain in the past, the longing for the way it used to be, ultimately led to division in the church.

How many times have we as the church been guilty of begging to grow, and when the increase came, we became uncomfortable with the stretching and the new ideas that didn't match our own status quo. We can so easily erect barriers and fail to make room for the new additions through our attitudes and complaining? If you bring new life into a closed system, adjustment is inevitable.

We have also seen this happen in unsaved families where the first member turns their life over to Jesus. There is a new "firstborn" in the family. It can cause a certain amount of stress as adjustments are made for the new life. Persecution and rejection are sometimes the result, especially when the family holds another faith.

Exploring the Spirit of Adoption

Chapter 4

Spiritual Parallels

Have you heard the stories—stories of adoptions gone sour, untold pain and anguish for families who have put it all on the line? Some families have given their all, only to experience the pain of a broken adoption relationship, unable to bring the healing needed for a successful outcome. The result is the relational equivalent of divorce. Known as "disruption," the adoptive child experiences separation from the security of a family once more. Once again, the effects of a perceived, if not actual rejection, have been impressed on the tender psyche of the child; like an emotional sliver in the spirit, to fester over time.

Wonderfully, there are more of the opposite—stories of adoptive children who have made great adjustments and were able to thrive in their new family environment. They've become valedictorian of their senior class or accomplished musicians, successful business people or healthcare professionals. In so doing, they have gone on to become vital and productive citizens. It is even possible to observe both scenarios within the same family.

A family may have two adoptive children from similar backgrounds, raised in the identical environment of loving, caring parents, yet one disintegrates emotionally and behaviorally while the other seems to thrive. This is not a situation restricted only to adoptive children. We see the same thing in biological families all the time.

Similar stories: Different outcomes

As a minister, I see the same phenomenon at work in the lives of those in the church. There can be two people with similar backgrounds, taught and discipled in similar fashion. One experiences victory in their personal walk with the Lord while the other experiences failure after disappointing failure.

A woman in our church, early in life, experienced childhood abuse followed by broken relationships with men as an adult. In spite of her broken history, she is the most peaceful, on fire, joyful and entertaining woman you would ever want to spend an evening with. I know another woman who has experienced similar circumstances in life. She is beaten down with a terrible self-image; consequently, she continues to return to the feeding trough of degradation and self-pity, again and again.

What's the difference? Both have had the experience of a similar environment, yet with drastically different results. Listen again to the words of the Apostle Paul:

For as many as are led by the Spirit of God, these are sons of God. For you did not receive the spirit of bondage again to fear, but you received the Spirit of adoption by whom we cry out, "Abba, Father." The Spirit Himself bears witness with our spirit that we are children of God (Romans 8:14-16).

One has received the Spirit of adoption and the other has not. One has cried out to Father, finding and receiving His love and the other is still searching for a father who will bring healing love, making it possible to have healthy relationships. Again and again, she finds it difficult to connect in healthy ways with others.

Issues of identity

In the world of adoption, attachment disorders can be common. These are often called "failure to bond" issues. While any adoptive child can exhibit symptoms, they are most often found in the child who has been severely neglected or where abuse is present. The atmosphere is one where those in authority who should have provided the most caring and nurturing of environments have instead, violated that sacred trust. It can also be present in the child where a bond has been formed and broken repeatedly.

This phenomenon exists because each one of us is created with a deep seated need to know the answers to three questions:

1. Who am I?
   Where, and to whom do I belong?
2. Where did I come from?
   What is my historical identity?
3. Where am I going?
   Given my circumstance, what is my potential?

The answers to these questions help to define one's sense of belonging. Every human being who has not found the answers to these questions will spend massive energy and resources, many times self-destructively, for one of two reasons. They are either trying to suppress emotional pain resulting from the lack of a sense of belonging, or they are engaged in an effort to find the safety and security afforded *by* the sense of belonging.

Do you know where you belong?

In my pastoral counseling office, there is a near constant stream of people who are desperately searching for the answer to these haunting questions. The emotional or relational symptoms presented are often different, but the root is readily recognizable.

As a society, we try to fill the emotional void by looking for love in all the wrong places: viewing pornography, addictions to fantasy-filled romance novels, filling our veins or noses with foreign substances, gorging our mouths with unhealthy food quantities or shopping till we drop (retail therapy). This is driven by a compulsive desire to find out who we are, to fill our insatiable need to know that we have worth and value as a human being. We will use practically any means to artificially medicate the pain of grief, loss, loneliness, abandonment, rejection or insecurity.

The driving need for a sense of belonging fuels the attraction to inner city gang activity. The gang is Satan's counterfeit to family. The Psalmist declares that God will set the solitary in families (Psalm 68:6), but this group of fatherless young people has settled for a destructive substitute. They have never experienced genuine family life, so they swallow Satan's substitute, doing whatever it takes to belong.

The needs of children

Every child is born with the basic emotional need for love and approval. In some institutional settings where children have been emotionally neglected and have never been shown affection through touch, the children have exhibited a failure to bond and in some cases, actually died from a lack of love! In a traditional, stable home atmosphere, moms and dads are present to care for, bond with, and provide for these basic needs. However, just being physically present is not enough. In the search for personal identity, I believe there are a couple of truths.

First, children receive a large portion of their gender identity from their father, or some other father figure, in their life. This is true for both males and females. In an emotionally and spiritually healthy environment, boys pattern after their father and learn what it is to be a man and how to treat others, especially the women in their lives, with respect and honor. They watch the way that Dad treats Mom. It has been said that the best gift a dad can give his children is to genuinely love their mother!

Children learn from the character of their fathers about providing for a family, both physically and emotionally. Fathers show the way.

Children learn from the character of their fathers about providing for a family, both physically and emotionally. Fathers show the way. Many individuals who engage in morally aberrant behavior have the common denominator of either an emotionally absent or aloof father in their history, or they have for one reason or another, broken off their relationship with him.

Interestingly, girls also receive a large part of their feminine identity from Dad. A girl who receives love, acceptance and approval from an emotionally caring dad, will seldom go looking for love "in all the wrong places." A dad who models love to his daughter, not for what he can get from her, but simply because of her worth and value as a person, can create in her a thirst for genuine relationships as she matures, not the broken substitutes so often offered as a counterfeit.

Interviews with girls who have prostituted themselves almost always reveal a broken or non-existent relationship with an emotionally unavailable dad. Prisons are filled with men and women who send thousands of cards on Mother's Day but rarely are more than a few Father's Day cards sent. So Dad, this points out that you are critically important in the life and development of your children, male or female, adopted or not!

Needed: Mothers who nurture

Secondly, Mom brings the incredible facet of security provided by nurture and care. Much has been written on bonding with Mom and the necessity of providing a safe environment for a child to grow and mature. This is especially true in the case of the adopted child. The primary bond has been broken and needs to be re-established. The tireless, unconditional love of a mom can create the seedbed for the new bonding to occur. This provides the absolutely essential soil into which fathers can sow.

Experience in observing a number of disruptions of children from adoptive families tells us that in most cases there has been a failure to bond between mother and child. A friend and his wife, who have adopted nearly thirty children over the years, mostly disruptions, have stated that they have found this to be the case in almost every one of their adoptions.

My purpose here is not to lay everything at the doorstep of the parents in the way of condemnation. All earthly fathers and mothers are imperfect and we often come short of being the ideal parent. However, I often give this counsel to individuals who have experienced difficult circumstances, perhaps even at the hands of their parents: their life is not the sum total of what has happened *to* them, rather it is the culmination of their *responses* to what has happened to them in their history.

Our wounded responses are a trap to us. They become sinful when they give way to bitterness and unforgiveness, bringing a life of pain as a result. The Apostle James writes that the way to healing is through confession, repentance and prayer (James 5:16).

Personal responsibility must be emphasized because healing from the wounding of the past never has to depend on the actions of another. Our environments have given us many and varied choices of response, but our way out of the brokenness, will always rest on our ability to forgive others and on our openness to receive the Father's love and forgiveness for ourselves.

Chapter 5

The Emotional Iceberg

When I traveled to Liberia to pick up our new son, Joshua, we were in the midst of a combat zone where ongoing civil war still raged. I noticed his hyper-alertness to all his surroundings, especially as we passed through the many military checkpoints positioned along the roadways. He carefully observed every gun, hand grenade and knife that the commandos carried. My first thought was, "This is an alert, bright little fellow...isn't that cute." I didn't realize, at that point, the alertness was the result of having been exposed, before the age of three, to the horrific atrocities of war.

Survival instincts were already deeply programmed into the mind and emotions of this young boy. It was only later, as the details spilled out, that we began to realize the possible depth of the experiences he had personally encountered. I recall one particular instance:

"Will they hurt the children?"

It was the spring of 1997. The carnage of another African insurrection was front page news. Scenes of horrible atrocities, replete with African insurgents dressed in camouflage and toting AK-47's spilled into our living room on the television news. These scenes were not unfamiliar to little three year old Joshua.

His question stopped me cold. I took him to another room, away from the visual reminders thrust upon us. The ensuing conversation revealed his exposure to the horrors of war, a very candid remembering of the decapitation of children and the discarding of their bodies.

The anger within

I knew where these children came from. Having traveled to Liberia four times in ministry, I had heard the stories; I had prayed with the victims. Everyone had stories of loved ones, friends, political figures, journalists; many brutally raped or murdered by drug-crazed, unremorseful combatants. But, this story…this story was now living in my house.

Over the next three years, his anger (seeded from the hurt caused by separation and insecurity) began to emerge, particularly when he perceived a sense of injustice. The anger was especially evident when Margaret and I attempted to leave him in the care of others. Separation anxiety would rise to the surface and Joshua would clearly illustrate his anger by throwing and breaking things or biting his caretaker. As painful as it was to go through this with him, it was absolutely essential that we repeat the cycle of leaving and returning, over and over again, until he learned that we would return. We found it helped his emotional state to leave a photograph of ourselves for him to focus on while awaiting our return.

Not all children come from war zones of course. By definition, all adoptees and foster children come from some sort of brokenness: an unplanned pregnancy, an unwed mother, a broken home, death of parents, drug or alcohol addicted parents, the product of incest or rape or the potential of having experienced sexual abuse. All these have a powerful effect on the formation of this person who is becoming a new addition to your family.

The effects of hyper-vigilance

Added to this historical baggage is the trauma of the transition. The child is now being removed from all that is familiar and is being placed into a loving, but very strange and new environment. I wrote earlier regarding the hyper-alertness I observed in Joshua while picking him up from Africa. Allow me a personal illustration to show how that can affect us. Not long ago, our phone rang at around 2 a.m. jarring us awake. On the other end of the line was an adult male voice growling in Satanic fashion, claiming to have killed others and was about to break into our home and kill us as well. As you can imagine, I did not sleep well for the next several nights and even got into a minor argument or two with Margaret regarding our course of action. We were on edge! My emotions were on hyper-alert and I was super vigilant in my awareness. Fortunately, the trauma soon passed as it was a one-time occurrence.

For many adoptive and foster children, this is a constant state of being. Imagine if you will, the deeper trauma of being totally uprooted from your familiar surroundings and placed in the care of totally unfamiliar people. The following fictional scenario someone once related to me may help further clarify a child's emotional perspective in this transition.

A parable

Imagine spending the first fifteen years of your life being told that when you grow up you are going to spend the rest of your life in Kansas. You spend all your time reading about Kansas, learning about Kansas, looking at pictures of Kansas and talking to every person you know who has ever been to Kansas, just so you can become more acquainted with your destination. The day arrives and you are placed on an airplane.

The plane takes off, but instead of going to Kansas, it arrives in Kenya. As you disembark, you are told this is where you will be for the rest of your life, never to return. You don't know the language or the customs. You don't know a single soul. Even though there are people waiting to greet you, you are abandoned, with no way to return, nor is there any means to communicate with the old and familiar. Your world has just spun out of control. You are no longer in touch with any kind of known reality. Panic, if not stark terror, begins to set in.

Does the imagery contained in this story give you some sense of the emotional turmoil that an adoptive child must face and have to work through? On occasion we have met with families at the airport as they receive the new addition to their family. As the escorts bring the children through the security gate and they meet their new family, they almost always have a sort of "deer in the headlights" look on their face. Many families simply do not realize that, like a partially submerged iceberg, the majority of swirling emotions these children are experiencing lie just under the surface.

Overwhelming intensity

Everything about this new world is foreign to them. The new sights, smells and tastes are radically different and accentuated, especially if this is an international or cross-cultural adoption. If the child is introduced into an existing family where other children are present, it will likely take a minimum of six months for the child to figure out where they belong in the new birth order.

The struggle to find were they fit can sometimes be quite painful. It is a world filled with insecurity and uncertainty. You will likely spend the bulk of your parenting years with this child, proving to them that there are relationships that can be trusted, that you won't go away like all the others, and that your love is unconditional, just like your heavenly Father's love for you.

The struggle to find were they fit can sometimes be quite painful. It is a world filled with insecurity and uncertainty.

Some approach adoption with the attitude that the adoptive child will just have to "fit in" with their routine. There is an unspoken expectation and belief that their family life will just be able to go on pretty much as normal. They are largely unaware of the tremendous emotional eddies, whirlpools and tidal waves that are at work in the heart of the child. One must become an expert in emotional jigsaw puzzles and detective work to ferret out the connections between the observed behavior and the underlying root causes that are functioning here.

Deciphering the signals

We have found there to be a window of opportunity that often seems to open up at bedtime. When you are tucking in your child, praying with them, there is a mental review taking place in the mind of the child. Out of this place of perceived safety, they will often begin to open up to you in that tender moment. Be very sensitive to the questions that come at this time. They are often loaded with much deeper thinking and emotion that lie hidden behind the initial sharing or questions at hand.

Exploring the Spirit of Adoption

Gentle probing may reveal the real reason they were obstinate that day, why they struck out at a sibling for no apparent reason or why they have been reported as having a struggle with misbehavior at school. Don't function in a sort of denial with your adopted child. Plan to be open about the adoption from the beginning and be willing to explore their world instead of expecting them to automatically accept and integrate fully into your world.

This child is different! He or she feels differently and thinks differently than your existing family. The challenge for the parent(s) is how to validate the feelings of the child while trying to minimize the differences that are present. There cannot be a differentiation of the expressions of your love between your biological children and adoptive children. In the event of an altercation between children, do the parents find themselves rising up in defense of the victimized child, or do they rise up to defend the biological status quo? The adoptive child is very quick to notice the difference. If you differentiate between your children in this way, you have just proven to the new child that they really don't belong and you have sown the seeds for failure.

In a recent conversation with an adoptee who is now a young adult, we were discussing the issue of receiving inheritance from ones parents. He is one of numerous adopted children in the family and was quite convinced that his adoptive parents would be leaving all of their estate to their biological children and he would basically receive nothing. It was very important to him that his adoptive siblings join him in purchasing the home place from the biological children when the time came, so they could have a connection to the only roots they had known. Whether this is the intent of the parents or not, it is the perception of the young man. Somehow he has gotten the message that he is second class as a child.

The importance of the birth order

As you plan for adoption, it is very important to consider the age of the adopted child in relationship to your other existing children. Disrupting the birth order, particularly of the first-born or oldest child, can potentially cause great difficulty. The displaced child can subconsciously begin to sabotage the integration of the new child into the family. I urge you to use great caution when choosing the age of the child you wish to adopt so you can avoid a great deal of heartache.

Not long ago we were presented with the possibility of adopting a boy who was three years older than our two adopted sons. Our boys were really gung-ho about the idea, even begging us to do so, until we sat down and asked the oldest if he was willing to give up being the oldest child at home. He thought through this for a moment and soon came to the conclusion that he didn't want his role to be supplanted in the family. I believe we avoided what could have been a painful set-up in our family.

What about you?

Have you ever felt like you didn't fit in? Maybe you have experienced abandonment, insecurity or uncertainty in your life. The circumstances I have been describing and the pain they cause, are not unique to adoption. Many of our inner city youth as well as others in their generation exhibit the very same symptoms. They are seeking an identity, to know who they are and to whom they belong. We see the rage generated by the abandonment suffered by many of these young people everyday in our newspaper headlines. Many have never experienced being close with another person that approaches any kind of relational health.

The same thing can apply to that new believer who just joined your church fellowship. He doesn't know the ropes yet. *"Doesn't he know how he is supposed to act? Some of those habits he has...someone needs to straighten him out if he expects to fit in here!"* I sometimes wonder who really needs the healing. Change, even in the best of circumstances, can challenge all of us with the adjustment it brings.

There is hope. There is a Father who can be trusted—One who awaits our coming to Him to receive the unconditional love and acceptance we all so desperately seek. Once we have received His healing touch, we can be conduits of His love to others who are hurting.

There is hope. There is a Father who can be trusted—One who awaits our coming to Him to receive the unconditional love and acceptance we all so desperately seek.

If a person is not secure in their relationship to Father or hasn't experienced and received His unconditional love, they may face a challenging time. Knowing that you belong *is* one of the deepest of human needs. It's true! He accepts all who call on His name. If you've gone through life feeling like you didn't quite belong, there is a Father in heaven waiting for you to call out to Him!

Chapter 6

The Fatherless

There is perhaps no greater, deeper or longer-lasting pain known to man than the emotional pain generated by issues of abandonment, rejection and betrayal. The ramifications in our society are staggering. I realize there is no such thing as a "pain" meter that can register emotional intensity and I understand that the emotional pain one experiences individually is uniquely his or hers.

It is my observation, however, that the results of fatherlessness, in all the forms it takes, are universally experienced. As author and conference speaker Gordon Dalbey communicates in his several books on the subject, we all have either absent or imperfect fathers. That being the case, we all have wounds inflicted that must be dealt with, brought into the light, and forgiven if we desire to live a life of wholeness.

Gordon once gave me a CD recorded by Brian Doerksen called *Father's House*. Included in the mix of primarily healing music is a song called, *We Are The Fatherless*. In stark fashion it exposes the rage resident within the hearts of many of our youth today as a result of the devastating emotional brokenness that comes from abandonment and rejection:

Can't trust no one, so I attack; ya better watch your step,
ya better watch your back
No, I'm not scared, I just push on; it's a ragged gang,
and it's where I belong;

I'm not, no I'm not, gonna let them hurt me again....NO!
No I'm not, no I'm not, gonna let them hurt me again;
Can you hear our cry, do you want the truth;
we're on the loose, and we're telling you;
We are... we are the fatherless!

Ya can't believe no one, it's a well known fact,
you better watch your mouth, 'cause I can kick right back
I'm a walking gun, a real life threat, can't count on
you, so I hedge my bets.[1]

Generational disconnection

Those of us who are of previous generations often dismiss
the youth of today and the message they bring. We brand them
as rebellious and antisocial. Many times there are elements of
both, so we give ourselves permission to ignore their cries in
cavalier fashion, because we are not willing to look at how we
may have had a hand in shaping this fatherless generation.

When we look at the consequences of our own generation's
response to parenting that resulted in the unfettered narcissistic
1960's, we see that the existence of the traditional nuclear family has taken a body blow, eliminating the safe haven needed
where children can grow up in a nurturing and caring atmosphere. "Free love," we cried. "No strings attached!" "If it feels
good, do it!" The inevitable "no commitment" life-style obliter-
ated the fabric of societal family relationships. Teenage preg-

nancy skyrocketed and divorce rates soared, giving rise to the fatherless generation to come.

I was amazed at what unfolded when I played Brian's CD for my then six year old adoptive sons. As soon as they got to that cut, they immediately sat up and took notice. Within one or two playings of the song it became their most requested number. It touched something deep within their hearts. Nowhere are the "father wounds" more clearly revealed than in the tapestry of events played out in the life of the adoptive or foster child.

As I stated in my introduction, these wounds are not unique to the adoptive or foster child, but they are usually exaggerated because of an almost universal sense of abandonment felt by these children. All of us, however, can point to wounding that stems from the unfortunate experiences of life. How do we achieve wholeness when we have experienced brokenness? Where does the power to live a restored life come from?

Jesus leads the way to healing

In Mel Gibson's movie, *The Passion of the Christ*, he portrays the last 12 hours of Jesus' suffering. In his depiction, Gibson includes the ongoing spiritual battle between light and darkness. Satan is represented by an androgynous creature, intricately involved in the event which stands at the apex of human history.

At one point in the movie, when Jesus is traveling the Via Dolorosa, carrying His cross, Satan is represented as holding and stroking a grotesquely deformed child in His arms. The point that Satan seems to be making is that *he* would never abandon *his* child like Jesus' Father did, mocking the Son of God for the path He had chosen. But then he is, after all, the father of lies.

The Bible tells us, that by the stripes Jesus received, He purchased our healing including all of our potential to come to wholeness. He was wounded for our transgressions…as well as the transgressions of our fathers! 2 Corinthians 5:21 tells us, *For He made Him who knew no sin to be sin for us, that we might become the righteousness of God in Him.* When Jesus "became sin" for us, He paid the full price necessary for our healing. When He "became sin" He also experienced the rejection and abandonment of His own Father.

When did Jesus begin to "become sin" for us? When did His Father turn away from Him? When did Jesus experience the stinging pain of fatherlessness? I believe it began in the Garden of Gethsemane. It was here that Jesus embraced the decision to "go it alone" in obedience to His Father. It was here that the pressure (Gethsemane means "an oil press") from the enormity of Jesus' decision caused Him to sweat as it were great drops of blood (Luke 22:44).

For the first and last time of all eternity, the Godhead experienced separation. It must have been agonizing, for both Father and Son. But Jesus had to fully drink the cup, even the cup of abandonment and separation, in order that we might have available to us, the healing grace needed to come to wholeness.

Who killed Jesus?

Nobody killed Jesus! Not the Romans; not the Jews, not even you and me! It is historically true that the Jewish authorities conspired against Him and turned Him over to the Romans.

It is also undisputed that the Romans physically crucified Him. God's Word makes it clear that all of our sins made Him the necessary substitutionary sacrifice on our behalf. It is also clear, however, that Jesus *chose* to suffer and die, and the death He suffered was by His own volition. As He told His disciples, not long before those final hours:

> Therefore My Father loves Me, because **I lay down My life** that I may take it again. No one takes it from Me, but **I lay it down of Myself.** I have power to lay it down, and I have power to take it again. This command I have received from My Father *(John 10:17-18 emphasis mine).*

The pages of this book focus on the heart of the adoptive child as a parable for the healing that we all need.

No one took Jesus' life from Him. He voluntarily laid it down, yielding His will to the Father's will. It was that willingness that purchased our healing and ultimate freedom.

Jesus cried out to His Father while on the cross, "*My God! My God! Why have you forsaken me?*" It was the ultimate cry of the human heart. It was the cry of one who was abandoned, one from whom His Father had turned away—the cry of one who had become sin, for you and me. Then, and only then, did Jesus declare the work finished and He chose to die. Right up to that point, He could have come down from the cross, but He chose to drink the full cup, for you and for me. He chose to be separated from His Father and in so choosing, made our restoration and reconciliation to the Father possible, never to be separated again.

The pages of this book focus on the heart of the adoptive

child as a parable for the healing that we all need. When we were born, we were born needing restoration to our Father. Original sin, and our cooperation with it, has stained us all and separated us from our Father who created us. Because we were born under the ownership of the evil one and all the brokenness that sin engenders, the Father, through Jesus, made a way for His children to be restored to relationship with Him by choosing to die.

Jesus overcame evil by being subjected to every temptation known to man and then triumphing over evil on the cross, retrieving the keys to hell and death. On the cross He destroyed the power of the enemy of our souls, setting the captives (you and I) free, making possible our adoption as sons and daughters of the Father.

There has been a dearth of fathering and mothering, mentoring and discipling that is now beginning to be recognized and addressed. Writers and ministers like John Trent, Larry Kreider, Gordon Dalbey and John Eldredge have been raised up in our generation to awaken us to our need and to help point the way to healing. We can gain valuable insight by taking a look at adoption and the lessons we can learn from those who have traversed the rocky path of breaking through the shell of the wounded heart.

> Forgiveness is the key to freedom. It is the key to healing. It is the key to leaving behind the pain of the past.

Forgiveness is the key

Jesus bore our pain and our shame on the cross and modeled the way to freedom and life. His freedom and ours, was wrapped up in one simple sentence as He hung on the cross, *"Father forgive them, for they don't know what they're doing"*

(Luke 23:34). His resurrection life depended upon it...and so does ours!

Forgiveness is the key to freedom. It is the key to healing. It is the key to leaving behind the pain of the past. It is the key to the restoration of all who have been abandoned, betrayed, wounded, offended, broken or rejected. To forgive is to simply say, "You don't owe me anything anymore!" It is to set the person free who has wounded you, to cancel the debt. Romans 12:17-19 spells out the principle:

Repay no one evil for evil. Have regard for good things in the sight of all men. If it is possible, as much as depends on you, live peaceably with all men. Beloved, do not avenge yourselves, but rather give place to wrath; for it is written, "Vengeance is Mine, I will repay," says the Lord.

There is insight in this scripture from which we can all benefit. When we choose to not avenge ourselves, to release the offender and forgive them, the Lord repays *us,* by healing us of our wounding which came by way of hurt and offense and restoring all the enemy has stolen through our brokenness. The Kingdom of God is upside down! He tells us to give in order to receive, return good for evil, bless when you are cursed and forgive in order to be healed!

The trap of the enemy

We must open up our hearts! That which is kept in darkness has power over us. When it is brought into the light and dealt with, it no longer controls us. Holding offense against another is self-defeating. It allows the hurt inflicted by the other person to continue to control the quality of our emotional and spiritual

Exploring the Spirit of Adoption

life! Every time we attempt to build relationship with others in the future, we will do so with a hardness in our heart that is caused by self-protectiveness. Our ability to be vulnerable will be truncated. Broken relationship after broken relationship will become self-fulfilling prophecies that are the result of the un-healed places of the heart.

This is the trap set by the enemy of our soul. If he can get us entrenched in the cycle of fatherlessness, generation after generation, he can keep us in a bondage of soul and spirit that not only compromises the individual, but can diffuse the effectiveness of the church as well as destroy the heart of a nation.

We are beginning to understand a little of what Paul meant by "receiving the Spirit of adoption." In the next chapter, we will look at one of the mechanisms in play that counteracts our ability to receive. Paul's words were purposefully chosen for a particular audience and they convey an understanding of a truth that could change your life.

[1] *We Are the Fatherless* by Brian Doerksen & Paul Janz –©1994 Father's House Publishing. Used by permission

Chapter 7

The Spirit of Rejection

"**M**r. Nice, your son has run away from school. A couple of teachers are trying to catch up with him but we'll need your help. He won't let anyone near him!" We had been experiencing a number of similar episodes in our home, but this was the first time it had spilled into the public arena.

When Daniel was around 18 months of age, first his father, then his mother disappeared into the jaws of the Liberian civil war after she dropped him off with an uncle. The uncle slipped across the border with Daniel and others into Guinea, to avoid attack from the rebels. Daniel fell sick and nearly died, no doubt due to malnutrition and rampant disease. After that, the uncle brought him to the African Christians Fellowship International orphanage in Monrovia, Liberia. Following recovery there, Daniel found himself, through the adoptive process, on his way to America.

One day our phone rang. On the other end of the line was an international director for PLAN Loving Adoptions Now, the adoption agency we had used when Joshua came to our home. "We have a situation where we need a family, preferably a family with other Liberian children. The family who brought him to America has decided they do not want him in their home any longer. You were the first on our list. Would you consider taking Daniel?"

After a four day "pregnancy" I was on an airplane to another state to pick up a boy who was being relinquished to PLAN on very short notice. When Daniel came to our home at the age of six, he was given the fourth name of his young life. He was passed from caretaker to caretaker in Liberia and only a year and a half after being adopted into a family in the United States, he was rejected by that family.

The rejected spirit

The spirit that stands in opposition to the Spirit of adoption is the spirit of rejection. I have written earlier about the importance of bonding to the new family. It is the spirit of rejection that stands in the way. The American Heritage Dictionary defines "reject" as: 1. To refuse to recognize, accept or make use of; to repudiate; 2. To refuse to grant or consider; deny; 3. To refuse recognition or affection to a person 4. To discard as defective or useless; to throw away; 5. To spit out or vomit.

There is something in all of us that wants to believe or expects, at a very basic level, that we should be spared hardship or injustice...that we should enjoy "protected" status from trial, misunderstanding or rejection. When that expectation is shattered, our hearts become a plowed field, vulnerable to the seeds of rejection. Once rooted, they are very difficult to weed out of our garden.

With rejection comes the closely allied spirits of bitterness and resentment. We see this in the creation story through the example of Cain. When he and his brother Abel brought their sacrifices to God, God accepted Abel's sacrifice because of the shed blood. Cain's sacrifice was rejected because it was produced out of the fallen earth, not acceptable to God. Because Cain did not learn and repent, his bitterness and resentment led to murdering his brother, Abel.

Our son Daniel has experienced a significant amount of rejection in his life. Before coming to our home he experienced numerous ways in which he felt ostracized from family life. These incidents were emotionally very devastating to him. After being in our home for approximately the same length of time he was in the previous home, he began to act out by running away, as well as in other ways.

These episodes were often tied together in cyclical fashion, occurring the same time of year over and over. Events like the time of year he arrived in the U.S. and Christmas were obvious triggers. Special events during the year are often triggers in the psyche of the adopted child. Holidays, birthdays and other significant times are a reminder to the child of the original family that should have been his or hers, giving rise to feelings of grief and loss. A particular trigger for children of adoption is when news of an adoption disruption reaches their ears. It stirs up the old familiar fear that was seeded by their own traumatic circumstances.

These sporadic episodes went on for about three years. For his own safety, and to break the cycle of rejection, we resorted to a very limited form of "holding therapy," literally holding him tightly but carefully, during his emotional meltdowns, until he processed those emotions. During these episodes of manifested rejection while he was screaming out, "I don't belong here, you're not my dad, you are all strangers to me, I hate you," I was speaking in his ear, "I'm your dad and you're my son and I'm not going anywhere." Slowly, over time, he is beginning to heal, and to believe that we can be trusted; that he will not be abandoned again.

It is a mistake to not look beyond the obvious behavior which normally cries out for discipline and try to discern the root cause. Behavior resulting from grief and loss cannot be corrected by normal disciplinary measures. The feelings of rejection must be drawn out and validated, and the child must be loved through the pain and not rejected again.

It is a mistake to not look beyond the obvious behavior which normally cries out for discipline and try to discern the root cause.

We are all vulnerable

At the age of four or five, I experienced a very small taste of what abandonment feels like, quite by accident. My family had traveled to a small eastern Oregon town for an overnight stay. While there, we drove a short distance to where a carnival was set up in town. It was my first experience with all the lights and activity. I was mesmerized and distracted by what was going on, so much so in fact, that I became separated from my parents for what seemed like an eternity. In reality it was only a few minutes, but extreme panic set in as I feverishly tried to find my family. I was lost and felt abandoned and alone.

This set up a series of events in my life, each reinforcing the previous event, that ultimately led to a stronghold of fear much later in life. The fear of abandonment and rejection will cause us to make decisions that can alter the course of our lives, veering us away from the plans and purposes God has for us.

A person that is laboring under a spirit of rejection could be defined as, "one who cannot receive love." This is a person who is convinced at a visceral level that, "you can't trust anyone." There is a self-protective mechanism that soon kicks into gear. It becomes a game of, "I'll reject you before you can reject me!"

As I stated earlier, the problem isn't what has happened to us, it is our *response* to what has happened. The seed of rejection is planted, sprouts, then grows, until the cycle of the "fear" of rejection is in full bloom. The original rejection, or repeated rejections, grow deep roots, producing automatic emotional and spiritual responses to anyone who tries to draw close.

If you cannot receive or accept love, then you cannot accept yourself as having worth and value, let alone love others.

If you cannot receive or accept love, then you cannot accept yourself as having worth and value, let alone love others! Jesus told us that we are to love others as we love ourselves. What a terrible bind that puts us into! If you cannot accept yourself or receive love from others including the Father's love, you cannot truly love God and experience the benefits of his love because as John wrote, *"We love God because He first loved us" (1 John 4:19).*

Do you know anyone like that? Their issues of abandonment and rejection are so strong that they can't form lasting relationships, rejecting anyone who gets too close. They literally don't like themselves because they feel they have no worth or value as a person. That has been proven to them over and over, rejection after rejection. Now, at the first sight of love, they run, not wanting to even countenance the possibility of another rejection.

The pain of rejection can be so intense that mental health professionals will tell you there are people who will bang their

Exploring the Spirit of Adoption

heads against the wall because the physical pain might distract them, if only for a moment, from the much deeper, more intense emotional pain that consumes them.

The acting out of rejection

As a pastor, I am encountering a phenomenon that is increasing in our world as a result of the self-hatred generated by the spirit of rejection. More and more people, teenagers in particular, are resorting to cutting themselves with various sharp instruments, or engaging in other types of self-abuse. They report a sort of "high"; a sense of release from the emotional pain they are experiencing.

Perhaps you have seen television shows or magazine articles depicting some of the extreme body modification and tattooing some have embraced. I have seen some who have turned their bodies into copies of reptilian creatures, complete with implanted spine ridges that resemble those of dinosaurs and large lizards. They are engaged in an empty search, looking for acceptance, some kind of reality that gives meaning to life. They hate themselves so much they are driven to transform themselves into a hideous likeness, anything that is other than who they are, trying to escape their pain.

There is only one antidote, the antidote of love brought to us by the Spirit of God. Romans 5:5 says:

Now hope does not disappoint, because the love of God has been poured out in our hearts by the Holy Spirit who was given to us.

The love of God, administered by the Holy Spirit is the only healing agent that can bring relief. Scripture also tells us that perfect love casts out fear. As we have noted earlier, it is the *fear* of rejection or abandonment that traps us in the place of poor decision-making in our lives. Adoptive children need a tremendous outpouring of the life and love of God. Even if they were adopted as infants, there will always be a need to deal with the "why" question of abandonment.

I was once talking with a friend who had been adopted as a small child. He told me all about his adopted parents and how they loved him. As I asked him if he ever felt like he struggled with being adopted he answered, "No, that's never bothered me at all!" He then proceeded to tell me about his teenage years of drugs, illicit sex, fighting and pursuing false religions. With his mouth, he was saying, "No, No," but with his actions he had loudly declared, "Who am I? Where did I come from?"

Examples in scripture

We have several examples in scripture where people experienced rejection. The first, our supreme example obviously, is Jesus. Listen to Peter's words in his first epistle, chapter 2:21-23:

For to this you were called, because Christ also suffered for us, leaving us an example, that you should follow His steps: Who committed no sin, Nor was deceit found in His mouth; who, when He was reviled, did not revile in return; when He suffered, He did not threaten, but committed Himself to Him who judges righteously.

The Bible tells us that although Jesus was reviled, (by definition had abuse heaped upon Him) He did not respond in like manner. Rather, He committed Himself (turned over the right to His own response) to His Father, and as a consequence, did not sin.

In the Old Testament, there are contrasting examples of how to respond. First, there was King Saul who found his identity in how he looked, how smart and how strong he was. He trusted in those attributes rather than God. He sought the approval of man rather than God. When God rejected him from being king over Israel, instead of repenting, he internalized that rejection and in fear, rejected all who followed after him, especially David. He was obsessed with pursuing David who was anointed to replace him as king, until he eventually died at the hands of the Philistines.

David, by contrast, followed the same path that Jesus later exemplified. He avoided Saul whenever possible, but when he had opportunity to reject the one who had rejected him, he spared his life. Even later on, when David had his own throne threatened by his sons and others, he did not reject in return, but left it in the hands of God to deal with. David knew what it was like to suffer rejection as a young boy, yet he chose to not become a "rejected person."

The seeds of rejection

I have seen the "spirit of rejection" often show up in church life. It manifests in what we sometimes call the "living together spirit." Many times, people take offense to things that have happened in their past church experience, giving entrance to the seeds of rejection which prohibits them from bonding with a body of believers. Committing to relationship within the church is almost outside their frame of reference, and many times, understandably so. The church, through its members, has often wounded and rejected many, inoculating them against receiv-

Many times, people take offense to things that have happened in their past church experience, giving entrance to the seeds of rejection which prohibits them from bonding with a body of believers.

ing the "Spirit of adoption," making it difficult to receive the Father's love for them. Consequently, they choose the path of "living together" in the church, never committing to covenantal relationship in one body. They move easily from church body to church body, never settling down for fear that betrayal will once again strike.

How then, shall we be delivered from this cycle which brings forth death? First, stop believing the lie! Proverbs 23:7 tells us, "For as a man thinks in his heart, so is he." What we think in our heart is based on what we believe. What we believe, is based in "whom" we believe. What are the lies of rejection that you have believed and who told them to you? Do you believe the sibling, the peer, the school teacher, who in a moment of frustration said hurtful things to you? What about a wounded parent that passed on generations of hurt through unkind words or emotional absence? Why not instead, choose to reject the lie?

Once, when I was about ten years old, I slid my hand along a wooden stake and acquired a sliver deep in the soft tissue between my thumb and forefinger. I pulled the sliver, thinking I gotten it all out. Over a year later, soreness developed in that hand. It started with just a little redness, and then it began to fester. After a few days, I finally screwed up the courage to poke at it with a needle and within a few minutes a fairly large sliver popped out along with the accompanying infection. Believing the lie brings with it a similar festering action in our emotional being.

There is an old saying, "time heals all wounds." I believe that to be untrue. Rather, "cleansing and closure heals all wounds." Time did not heal the sliver in my hand. Ignoring the pain and unresolved feelings associated with a hurtful word or circumstance will not bring freedom from the infection of re-

Exploring the Spirit of Adoption

jection. Only by forgiving the offending party and in choosing to believe the truth will there be relief and victory over the rejection that has taken root in your heart. Believing the truth is the second step to freedom.

We should note here, that the truth is not a set of beliefs or a body of knowledge. The truth is a person. His name is Jesus. He is the Word, come in the flesh. Therefore if we meditate on the scriptures and what they have to say about us, we will get an understanding of who God says we are. Scripture passages like these let us know that we have not been rejected by Him and that He has accepted us.

> Only by forgiving the offending party and in choosing to believe the truth will there be relief and victory over the rejection that has taken root in your heart.

Ephesians 1:3-6:

*Blessed be the God and Father of our Lord Jesus Christ, who has blessed us with every spiritual blessing in the heavenly places in Christ, just as He chose us in Him before the foundation of the world, that we should be holy and without blame before Him in love, having predestined us to adoption as sons by Jesus Christ to Himself, according to the good pleasure of His will, to the praise of the glory of His grace, **by which He made us accepted in the Beloved** (emphasis mine).*

Isaiah 41:9:

*You whom I have taken from the ends of the earth, And called from its farthest regions, And said to you, You are My servant, **I have chosen you and have not cast you away** (emphasis mine).*

Jesus was the most rejected man to ever walk the face of the earth, yet He was not a rejected person. Even in His final hour, His own Father turned away from Him because He *became* sin for us. He took upon himself the wrath of God poured out against all sin, on our behalf. Why was He victorious over rejection? It is revealed in some of His final words. "Father, forgive them!"

The scriptures are full of examples of rejection and how men dealt with it. Usually, there was a dynamic encounter with the living God. I already wrote of David and his response. Moses was raised a fatherless man who tried to overcome his rejection and the rejection of his people by the arm of the flesh. It basically got him turned into a desert rat...until he had an encounter with God. Then he became Moses the Deliverer.

Jacob was certainly a man with rejection issues. He spent a good part of his life wanting to be his brother, desperately trying to get the birthright (father's approval) by the arm of the flesh through deceitful means. At Peniel, which means "facing God," Jacob had an encounter with the living God and never walked the same again! He was restored to his brother, Esau, as well. I once heard a precious brother in the Lord say, "Never trust a man who doesn't walk with a limp!"

The Apostle Paul was a man breathing threats and dire consequences against all believers when he had an encounter with God on the Damascus Road. His life change has influenced all of human history. When you have an encounter with the Lord, you will never walk the same either!

John, "the disciple Jesus loved," writes that knowing and receiving the truth brings us into freedom. How great is our deliverance when we get hold of the truth. What a freedom to be released from the bondage and effects of rejection. Of a certainty, it is the truth (Jesus) that makes us free.

Chapter 8

Beware the
Identity Thief

G od has a plan and purpose for the life of every individual. Jeremiah 29:11 makes that abundantly clear to us.

For I know the thoughts that I think toward you, says the LORD, thoughts of peace and not of evil, to give you a future and a hope.

His thoughts for us have been formulated and developed since eternity past. He knew us before we were even formed in our mother's womb. His desire is to see the fulfillment of all He has purposed for us.

We also have an enemy and Satan has a different plan for our lives. He wants to disrupt God's plan and calling for our lives through the hurt and wounding of rejection and abandonment. As I stated earlier, the quality of our life is determined, not by what has happened to us, but by our *responses* to what has happened to us. The enemy of our souls is expert in setting up potential emotional trapdoors, baiting us to take a step towards resentment or bitterness, trapping us in our responses and judgments with one purpose in mind. He wants to take your life!

John 10:10 sets up the scenario for us:

The thief does not come except to steal, and to kill, and to destroy. I have come that they may have life, and that they may have it more abundantly.

His purpose is clear and his methodology is predictable. Satan wants to depress us so that he can oppress us. Oppression leads to possession which then leads to death. He hates the Spirit of adoption, the plan of the Father which gives a new personal and family identity to all who embrace it. Thankfully, the nullifier of Satan's plan is contained in the same verse. Jesus is all about life and living it to the full.

Stealing the identity

One of the predominant ways I have seen Satan attempting to accomplish his diabolical goal is through the stealing of an adopted child's identity. Many times in a difficult adoption situation, in order to look for explanations as to why things are going wrong, the parent(s) begin a search, looking for reasons why this particular child is the apparent source of so much pain in their family. There is a temptation to quickly begin labeling the child. Sometimes it is out of desperation or sometimes it is driven by the need to deflect attention away from their own lack as parents. Perhaps they were not prepared emotionally for the long haul, perhaps their own history of hurt and wounding play a part, rendering them ineffective in keeping a clear perspective about the situation at hand.

In situations like these, we have seen role reversal often take place as the parent responds in anger towards the child. The parent becomes childish in their own responses and expects the child to act like an adult even though they are incapable of doing so. The need to blame sometimes surfaces and that's where the labeling begins.

We have many labels to choose from today. What I am about to say should not be taken as a disparaging of genuine diagnosis, but in our information age it is easy to take exaggerated childish behavior and immediately look for symptoms to back up our suspicion that this child is somehow emotionally or mentally defective. Disorders such as ADHD (Attention Deficit Hyperactivity Disorder) and RAD (Reactive Detachment Disorder) have been popularized in our culture to the point that almost any evidence of childish disciplinary issues or high energy can be blown out of proportion making labeling and medicating an easy answer. It has the effect of diverting the attention away from potential issues with our parenting skills, our adoptive preparation or our inability to cope with the difficulty at hand.

Behavioral triggers

With adoptive or foster children there is sometimes an errant expectation that this child will automatically respond and act like the secure and cared for biological child. For example, in international adoptions as well as situations of domestic neglect, food often plays a major role in the emotional demeanor of a child. We have seen this effect over and over: a child begins to misbehave and no amount of reasoning seems to yield any benefit. Sit down to a meal and within minutes the whole world has been set right again. Delaying a meal for most of us yields very little, if any, trauma. For the neglected child, or one with a history of malnutrition, it is huge. The security represented by the presence of abundant food is paramount to their well being.

Our normal response is to jump into disciplinary mode, rather than discerning the true need of the child.

Adoptive children are an easy target. Their identity is already a question of concern for them. If the enemy can get us to label a child falsely, he has taken the first major step in stealing that child's identity. We have seen several cases where this has been in evidence: a child who was labeled as deficient mentally regarding their ability to learn, who is now excelling academically in a new family; another very young child who was falsely accused of touching a child inappropriately who now has a tremendous ministry with children through teaching Sunday School at a variety of levels; a third child who has strong leadership potential accused of being a "little Hitler" and the list goes on.

It breaks my heart when I see children, before they have even begun to explore their potential, labeled, branded and rejected. It is almost never done intentionally. The parents are at their wits' end, feeling they have exhausted every avenue of hope. Having failed to find an easy explanation for their child's behavior, the search for a label begins. Divide and conquer is the tactic of the enemy. If he can get the parents to emotionally detach, to emotionally disown the child, he has won the battle if not the war.

The nature is in the name

Revelation 2:17 gives us a hint as to the Father's redemptive purpose:

To him who overcomes...I will give him a white stone, and on the stone a new name written which no one knows except him who receives it.

We find in scripture that the identity or nature of a person is closely tied with their name. God often gave new names to people when they received a nature change. Abram became Abraham, Sarai became Sarah, Jacob became Israel, Cephas became Peter and so on. A new identity accompanied these people as God changed their hearts and circumstances. A name is also a label. Take care in the choosing of your adopted child's name. It does have meaning and significance.

> We find in scripture that the identity or nature of a person is closely tied with their name. God often gave new names to people when they received a nature change.

There is also a "calling forth" that occurs when a new name is given. There is a period of time that often occurs as the person grows into the meaning of the new name. If a child is called "stupid" over and over again he will grow to adopt that identity about himself. Imagine if you called your child "sweetheart" or "a blessing" or "smart" or "gentle." How might the result be different?

I have a friend who is on her fourth legal name. Early names in her life were associated with wounding, hurt and abuse. As an adult she changed her first name to reflect the person she was becoming and wanted to become, leaving behind the identities of earlier years. Calling forth a new identity in adoptive children is of utmost importance, helping to give them an emotionally stable and secure foundation.

In the quest for identity and security, an adopted child will often have questions about why they had to leave their family or country of origin. Comfort is found in directing our attention once again, back to the scriptural evidence of how Father often works.

The plan of God

Many times in the Bible, God removed a child or young person from their surroundings in order to accomplish His higher purposes. One need only think of Moses who was adopted into Pharaoh's family on the way to becoming the deliverer of Israel. Samuel was removed from his home to be raised in the temple on his way to becoming a judge and prophet in Israel. How about Joseph—sold into slavery then positioned to provide famine relief to the people of God, rising to the rank of second in command in all of Egypt? Naaman was grateful for the captive Hebrew servant girl who told him of a prophet in Israel who could heal him of his disease. Ruth, Esther and others were displaced from their roots to become key figures in the spiritual economy of God.

God has a purpose for every child. We dare not become complicit with the enemy in his desire to destroy identity. We have the wonderful opportunity to call forth the true nature that God has placed in each of His children. It is a battle worth fighting. It is absolutely life changing in its implications. Don't be deterred or become weary in well-doing!

Chapter 9

Adoption—
Contract or Covenant?

I feel it is important to include a chapter on the understanding of the difference in "covenant" and "contract" regarding the issue of adoption. I have seen families go through disruption after adopting because of, I believe, an errant understanding or application of the principles of covenant. The approach taken in relationship to adoption can make or break the potential success of this new adventure.

In the town where I live, there are subdivisions that have a list of requirements that one must follow if you are to gain permission to build in that neighborhood. These requirements, called "covenants," are above and beyond the basic code requirements that are enforced by local inspectors for any other normal construction.

Generally, these covenants are a set of agreements that, by someone's definition, will enhance the beauty, longevity or livability of a house in that particular area or conforms to the style that reflects the surrounding housing environment. When you hire a contractor to build your house in this area, you will sign a "contract" with him that spells out the construction and financial terms of the project.

A successful adoption will integrate both of these ideas in the formation of the new relationship. You will have a contract with an agency or attorney that will spell out the specific details of your adoption. These details will include, but are not limited to, financial arrangements, home study requirements, criminal background checks, pre-adopt education and how or when the child will be transferred to your custody.

Contracts are defined as the exchange of property, time, services or commodities for financial considerations. In adoption, contracts are necessary to cover the legalities involved in order to complete the adoption. We have discovered, because our boys are of African descent, that this aspect can be a stumbling block for some Americans who are of African descent. Because our American history includes the insult and horror of slavery, paying an agency or an attorney for the services to adopt a child, especially a black child, for some, can be a painful reminder of our infamous past.

How contracts and covenants differ

Covenants on the other hand, as they apply to people, are the exchange or gift of personhood from one to another. Covenant involves a shared bond between individuals. Ancient covenants were characterized by several components. First, there was a list of the parties involved followed by the terms of the covenant. Contained within the terms was a list of the blessings and curses that would follow the individuals if they chose to keep or abandon the terms of the covenant.

God initiated such a covenant with Abraham. (You can read about it in Genesis, chapter 15.) Contracts and covenants share the common aspect that if the terms are broken, consequences will result. This however is where the similarities end. Contracts can be fulfilled or completed or they can be broken or revoked. Covenants, between individuals however, can be kept, abandoned or superceded by a better covenant.

The depth of "covenant"

We have several examples of covenant in the scriptures that shed light on the seriousness of covenant. Once again, David and Saul, and we'll include Jonathan this time, serve as our examples. To understand the interplay, we have to go back in history four hundred years earlier.

When Joshua and the Israelites crossed the Jordan River into the land promised to them by God, they began to have military success. As they took more and more land, their fame began to go before them. A group of people called the Gibeonites, fearing they were next in line to be conquered, dressed themselves in rags, carried with them moldy bread and misrepresented themselves to the leaders of Israel. They claimed to have come from a far country when, in reality, they were from just over the next hill!

The Gibeonites entered into a covenant with Israel. The terms stated they would receive Israel's protection from all their enemies and in exchange they would become servants to Israel. When the Israelites discovered they had been deceived, they were angry. However, because of their understanding of covenant, they were bound to the terms. Scott Hahn, in his book, *A Father Who Keeps His Promises* (page 26), describes the ancient understanding of covenant in this way:

For ancient Israelites, a covenant differed from a contract about as much as marriage differed from prostitution. When a man and woman marry, they declare before God their undying love to one another until death, but a prostitute sells her body to the highest bidder and then moves on to the next customer. So contracts make people customers, employees, clients; whereas covenants turns them into spouses, parents, children, siblings. In short, covenants are made to forge bonds of sacred kinship.

In Israel, a marriage between man and woman had three parts; the negotiated agreement, the betrothal and the ceremony. The difference between our modern day engagement and their betrothal was that the betrothal was a time of testing of the bride for purity and could only be broken by death or divorce. It was considered a part of the covenant between them. Jesus is also pursuing a tested bride, one that will be found without spot or wrinkle.

Four hundred years after the Gibeonite covenant was entered into, two things happened. First, Saul's son, Jonathan, entered into covenant with David. It was a friendship covenant that bound them to walk together in relationship, with Jonathan agreeing to stay by David's side and David always having a kindness for Jonathan's descendants.

In my view, Jonathan seemed to abandon his covenant with David by choosing his father's house over David's house, eventually costing him his life on the battlefield. After Jonathan's death, David cared for Mephibosheth, Jonathan's crippled son, guaranteeing him a place at David's table for the rest of his life.

The second thing to happen was that while Saul was king, he slew a certain number of Gibeonites in violation of the protection clause of the first covenant. After David became king, a famine had enveloped the land. When he sought the Lord for the reason for the famine, he discovered Saul's sin was the cause. In his desire to repair the breach of the covenant, he asked the Gibeonites what they required as restitution. As a result, he agreed to turn over seven of Saul's descendants to be hanged by the Gibeonites. In order to keep both covenants, he turned over descendants that were not of the house of Jonathan. So David understood the need to keep covenant, even a covenant begun in deception four hundred years earlier.

> David understood the need to keep covenant, even a covenant begun in deception four hundred years earlier.

The adoption covenant

So what does this have to do with the Spirit of adoption? A family who enters into adoption with a "contract" mindset that does not extend beyond the legalities into covenantal relationship, will run a high risk of disruption because they will view the brokenness of the child and the emotional difficulties that arise, as a breaking of the "contract." They then give themselves emotional permission to reject or "disrupt" the child on that basis.

Families that do not expect to adjust to the new child are not entering into covenant with flexibility. What are the needs of the new child? What if he or she upsets the status quo of your life? (That's a guarantee!) How will you respond? I have heard adoptive parents say, "We can't do this!" or "We can't do that!" In reality, many times "can't" often means "won't."

Needs of the child come first

What if you home school and your child needs the interaction of other children, having come from an orphanage situation? Can you bend to the child's needs? What if your child struggles in a classroom setting, not yet ready for mainstreaming? Can you allow for an alternative solution? I am aware of a situation where a family adopted cross-culturally. The mother is a school counselor, yet they chose to disrupt the child from their home in a very short time, because they apparently were unwilling to make the required life-style adjustments.

As I mentioned earlier, when things begin to deteriorate, we have often seen that the parents will begin to expect the child to act like the adult in the relationship. They expect responses from the child that would be difficult for a healthy adult, let alone a child who has been broken by the circumstances of life.

When biological children are born into a family, there is an emotional bonding between parent and child. You would never consider giving up your child because they were difficult in some way or strong-willed. Adoption is, at its best, a covenantal relationship, initiated by the parent. Many families, especially in international adoption, encounter situations where the information received about the child is faulty. Maybe the child has an illness that was not previously known. Perhaps they are a different age than you were led to believe by the foreign nationals responsible for their care. Many times, accurate and thorough background information is simply not available, especially for children of war.

Remember the Gibeonite covenant, founded on deception! If your biological child were born with a heart defect, would you immediately consider giving up your child? Of course not! You must consider the consequences of entering into covenant with a child before taking the plunge. They are not a suit off the rack that you can return if they don't fit. They must be treated as if they are actually your child, because once you receive them, they are!

Exploring the Spirit of Adoption

Before anyone who is having a difficult time or has experienced disruption falls into condemnation, please allow me to say something about adoptions that genuinely don't work out. I stated earlier that there was one way that a covenant could be changed. Until Jesus came, God's people were under the Old Covenant [testament]. Jesus ushered in a new covenant that the book of Hebrews tells us was a "better covenant." An old covenant can be superceded by a better covenant. Sometimes, for a variety of reasons, a family is not prepared, educationally, emotionally, culturally or spiritually for what they encounter in an especially difficult adoption.

There are families that are called by God, skilled and prepared to enter into a better covenant for that child. Obviously, all avenues should be tried in order to preserve the original covenant, but when disruption occurs, there is a way to healing, for both the family and the child.

Father has initiated and entered into a covenant with you. He isn't going anywhere. He has promised to never leave you or forsake you. The Father's heart is to heal and to restore. This is the goal of the Spirit of adoption. The Father's heart is for the broken, the downtrodden, the abandoned, and the rejected. His heart is for you!

Chapter 10

The Love of a Father

My father is like many of your fathers. He is a product of the depression, from a generation of people who have experienced more change in their lifetimes than any other generation in the history of the world. Post World War II, this generation single-handedly produced, at great personal sacrifice, arguably the greatest and most affluent society ever known to man.

This protector/provider generation was adept at caring for the physical needs of their families but, when it came to emotional expressions of love, found it hard to find the words. You know the old double-edged joke, "I told you once that I love you; if I ever change my mind, I'll let you know!"

Dr. Gary Chapman, in his book, *The Five Love Languages*, lays out for us five different ways we humans express and receive love. These five ways include:

1. Words of affirmation or encouragement
2. Acts of service
3. Gift giving
4. Quality time
5. Physical touch

We all tend to have one or two ways that are at the top of our list. For my wife it is acts of service. For me, it is words of affirmation. This simple discovery has added a wonderful dimension to our relationship and the ways we show our love for one another. It is critically important to recognize the languages of love our children employ, to better communicate our love and approval to them. This is especially true of the adoptive or foster child.

Judgment arises out of ignorance

My father operates in the arena of gift-giving and acts of service. Can you see the set-up between my father and me? Growing up, I desperately wanted to hear words of encouragement, words of affirmation that communicated my father's approval of me. There was a conflict between my head and my heart. I knew with my head that my father loved me, but my heart was unconvinced, so much so in fact, that as I grew older, I became mired in an emotional wounding that he was not even aware of. Somewhere in the core of my being, I had begun to hold my dad hostage emotionally. Internally, I was demanding that he express his approval and love for me on my terms and if he did not do so, I judged him less than adequate as a father.

About twelve years ago, I recognized my sin of judgment. I confessed this sin to my adoptive heavenly Father and I released my dad from ever having to communicate his approval to me on my terms. I told my heavenly Father that His approval was enough for me, and it was to him that I would go for my words of affirmation.

Blessing comes with releasing

Several days later, immediately following this release of my father, I had an amazing experience. We are a family that enjoys hunting as a pastime. For the last 28 years my brothers and I, along with our Dad, have spent a week together hunting elk; a male bonding experience to say the least! This is a tradition that has been, and is being, passed down to our sons.

Until this particular year, Dad had not been successful in harvesting an elk and I had been praying for his success for several years. As I was driving down a forest road, I looked out my window to see a herd of elk just a hundred yards away. I exited my truck, got into position and filled my elk tag. It was just that simple. It was the fourth year in a row I had been successful. After checking the animal, I began to get frustrated with God and I cried out to him almost in anger, "Why did you give me an elk and not Dad?" I heard the voice of the Lord in my heart, as clearly as I've ever heard Him, "Because I'm your Father and I wanted to, because I love you!"

> **Because of my judgments, I had blinded myself to receiving his language of love. He had been telling me of his love and approval all along, and I just couldn't see it or fully receive it!**

Suddenly, memory after memory began to wash over me of how my dad had given me various gifts over my lifetime, showing his love for me. Because of my judgments, I had blinded myself to receiving his language of love. He had been telling me of his love and approval all along, and I just couldn't see it or fully receive it!

I received a new revelation of my heavenly Father that day as well. He delights in His children! He loves to bless and if we don't judge him as less than adequate, as distant and difficult to reach, our spiritual eyes will be opened to the healing love that is readily available. He loves us with an everlasting love, fully and completely.

Exploring the Spirit of Adoption

How often are we captive to the bondage of our own judgments? Our disappointment with life is fueled by our unfulfilled expectations. Unable to see through the eyes of another, we judge their actions and words towards us as deficient. We take offense, and in the process bind ourselves to deep wounding and pain.

Discovering the roots of anger

So many relationships disintegrate under the weight of angry exasperation. I have learned to trace backwards to find the root cause of the anger. If you look under anger, you will find some kind of hurt. Under hurt is disappointment with another person or the circumstances of life and under disappointment you will find unfulfilled expectations. Here is where judgments of another begin. Somebody let you down! They didn't act or respond the way you wanted them to. We then judge and condemn their hearts…something we can't fully know. The enemy of our soul moves in to sow his seed in the fertile ground of disappointment. As he is the father of lies, only spiritual death can result.

Can you see the application here of what happens in the heart of the fatherless? The expectation is for a normal, nurturing life. There is plenty of opportunity for unfulfilled expectation to provide fuel to the fire of brokenness. But, Father God waits patiently for us to come to Him. He has the healing of a Father's love, and He often dispenses it through earthen vessels like you and me.

Healing the fatherless

Several years ago on Easter Sunday, a very dear friend, a lady in our congregation, went home to be with the Lord after a long and protracted illness. Through this process, I became acquainted with her son, Steven, age 29 at the time. He had not been involved with church during his adult life, at least partly due to wounding received as a child in the midst of a church situation. Over the course of that year, Steven and I began to build a relationship together. When she passed away, Steven's mother took the identity of Steven's father to the grave with her. She had never married and had raised him as a single mother.

During the year following his mother's death, Steven, a devoted husband and father, began searching for direction and purpose for his life. A few months later he decided to join the military, serve his country and receive medical training in hopes of becoming an EMT. When Steven was about to graduate from boot camp, I felt a prompting of the Lord that I should fly to Fort Knox, Kentucky, to participate as substitute family.

Steven didn't know I was coming and it was to be a surprise. The night before graduation, I was praying and asking the Lord, "What should I say to him when I see him?" This is what I felt I was hearing from God and subsequently said to him. "Steven, this is a time when a dad ought to be here. If you would let me stand in that place for just a moment, I'd like to tell you that I'm proud of you!"

Some time later, his wife told me that after boot camp, while Steven was in the hospital fighting pneumonia, the army chaplain visited him, asking him if he had any parents. Steven told him, "My mother passed away a year ago, and I met my father for the first time!" His comment was in reference to our new found relationship, begun in the ashes of grief, following the death of his mother. This experience has opened my eyes to the broad spectrum of possibilities we have to minister to the fatherless.

Opportunities to minister to the fatherless come in many forms. Many have suffered at the hands of abusive dads or moms.

Many have grown up just like Steven, never knowing his biological father. Others have been torn from all that is familiar, separated from family by war, accident or calamity. We have a generation of inner city youth who live with their mothers, having been abandoned by their fathers. They are often filled with pain and rage.

The way back

But, good news! God has a plan, and it is not plan "B"! The Spirit of adoption was God's original plan. He did not come up with this plan in a desperate last ditch attempt to salvage this world. Revelation 13:8 speaks of the, "Book of Life of the Lamb slain from the foundation of the world." The foreknowledge of God led Him to put in place a redemptive plan before the creation of man. This means that God knew that in order for man to love God out of freedom he had to have a choice. He also knew that man, through Adam, as a result of that choice, would fall from grace.

Part of His plan from the very beginning was to pour out the Spirit of adoption as a redeeming action, to reconcile man to Himself. It was not only through our own spiritual adoption or the adoption of literal orphans, but that we might father the fatherless wherever we encounter them, and recognize the universal need of the Father's love in the heart of every man, woman and child. There is much at stake in our world. Malachi chapter 4:5-6 gives us a warning as well as a promise:

> *Behold, I will send you Elijah the prophet before the coming of the great and dreadful day of the LORD. And he will turn the hearts of the fathers to the children, and the hearts of the children to their fathers, lest I come and strike the earth with a curse.*

A land that ignores the fatherless does so at great peril. We have been given a great promise, the promise that it can be done, the promise that the power of love is greater and when released, will bring blessing to the land.

A father of the fatherless, a defender of widows, is God in His holy habitation. God sets the solitary in families; He brings out those who are bound into prosperity; But the rebellious dwell in a dry land (Psalms 65:5-6).

When King David penned these words, they displayed the heart of someone who had experienced, not only the acceptance of a loving and forgiving heavenly father, but also hinted at an intimate knowledge of the pain of one who has felt the sting of being fatherless. Why didn't his father initially call him, as one of his sons, to Samuel's anointing service for a new king? Why didn't he measure up? Was there more behind his words from Psalm 51:5, "I was brought forth in iniquity and in sin did my mother conceive me," than the obvious allusion to original sin? Was he of questionable parentage, born in shame? I wonder!

We have been given a great promise, the promise that it can be done, the promise that the power of love is greater and when released, will bring blessing to the land.

To be certain, his experiences with Saul as a substitute father figure left something to be desired. Yet, he forsook the dry land of the rebellious and embraced the Father who brings us all, from bondage to liberty and from emotional want to loving prosperity, if only we will allow him.

This is my prayer for you, *to know the love of Christ which passes knowledge; that you may be filled with all the fullness of God (Ephesians 3:19).*

Chapter 11

Issues of Discipline

There is probably no question I receive more than some form of the following: "So I have a special emotional needs child; how do I bring discipline and order into their lives?" These children exhibit many different, sometimes contradictory, behaviors as they process their feelings. There is the silent "refusal to talk" child, the running away child, the combative child, and the list goes on. How does one minister to the unique needs of the adopted or foster child?

If you endure chastening, God deals with you as with sons; for what son is there whom a father does not chasten? But if you are without chastening, of which all have become partakers, then you are illegitimate and not sons (Hebrews 12:7-8).

It is clear from scripture that to neglect the disciplining of our children is to communicate a lack of care for them and the lack of sense of value to be placed on them. We as parents are charged with this responsibility and it is an expression of love to do so. It is also imperative to recognize that methods and understandings that may be effective with well-adjusted biological children may not be adequate to address the needs of the struggling child. Clear boundaries and predictable structure provide the necessary security and safety they need for a healthy environment. While this is true for all children, it is especially so for adoptive and foster children.

This must be the foundational understanding of our interaction with the adoptive or foster child. They are programmed differently due to life's circumstances and their journey to emotional health presents new and different challenges. Basic Biblical principles of love, acceptance, patience and tolerance are an obvious must that should be applied universally to all children, but especially to these children with their heightened struggle.

Exercising flexible discipline

Traditional methods of discipline are often inadequate to address the needs that arise. Just modifying the behavior for the moment yields only temporary results. An underlying biblical principle I have found to be helpful is teaching the child, through the process of discipline, to understand the reason "why" the behavior is unacceptable. Jesus told us that all of the law and prophets hang on two simple understandings, loving God and loving others. All our behaviors have effects that go beyond ourselves, impacting others within our circle of influence, as well as our relationship with God. It is needful that this be the beginning point and focus of our disciplinary process.

The goal in discipline is for the child to become self-governing in their behavior. That being the case, it is the heart that needs adjustment, not just the behavior. If we only adjust behavior, as soon as the child is out of sight, they return to that which is unprofitable. These children will sometimes interact in ways that defy normal disciplinary action. They often do not have typical response mechanisms in place and so require extra time and patience to establish the norms. Sometimes it seems these children are deep "emotional black holes" which, no matter how much love you pour in, are never filled up. Do not become weary in well doing! Except in cases of the most severely damaged, love eventually begins to win out.

It's not about you!

One of the greatest traps for parents of special emotional needs children is the feeling that they [the parent] have somehow been personally violated by the behavior of the child. If the parent gets drawn into the conflict and feels personally wounded by the child's actions, they are no longer able to administer proper discipline. As parents, we must rise above the conflict and understand that we are the adult, capable of separating fact from emotion. The child often does not yet have that capacity. If you are attempting to discipline out of anger, it is time to back off.

If you have parented biological children, you already know that different children respond differently to discipline. One child may respond immediately to just being spoken to while another needs much stronger forms of discipline. Most children need to experience the safety of strong and enforced boundaries as this communicates love and care to them.

One must learn to separate the scriptural term "foolishness" which arises out of rebellion, from "childishness" which is the result of immaturity. A third source of misbehavior comes from the brokenness of a traumatic history. Each of these requires a different disciplinary approach. In the first case, foolishness must be met head-on with appropriate discipline. In the second case, there are many times when children who misbehave out of childishness are mistakenly punished as if they were in rebellion. A greater focus and emphasis on the natural consequences to their behavior is more effective in bringing about the desired result. The spilled milk or the broken lamp caused by uncontrolled energy must be cleaned up and/or paid for.

Other common issues that can contribute to childish behavior are the immediate need for food or rest. We have seen incredible instantaneous changes take place in the emotional expressions of our boys, as well as other children, in the first few minutes of a meal. In particular, children who come from a history of malnutrition or other forms of deprivation are affected by this. Food represents security and relief from pain. Their internal emotional responses take a greater toll on them than what you would normally experience, necessitating the security provided by supplying their bodily needs. The source of the misbehavior can potentially be misinterpreted causing the child to be unduly disciplined when perhaps all they need is to be fed!

Finally, the third type of child is one who has experienced significant issues of rejection and will interpret harsh punishments as further rejection rather than redemptive love. Sending some of these children to their rooms may further cement their belief that they are not loved, wanted or accepted. Consequences that encourage continued interaction with the family help to counteract the feelings of rejection.

Power and control

Some children will attempt to engage in open power plays designed to gain control. Muttering under their breath or open verbal expressions are sometimes best met with complete ignoring of the behavior. This removes the reward and ultimately the motivation for the action. Stomping up the stairs begs for unhealthy attention from the parent. Ignoring it often makes it a very unrewarding and unfulfilling action. Talking it through later, after the pressure has subsided, turns it into a teaching opportunity instead of a disciplinary one.

There may be times when some children will express their inability to cope emotionally by running away. It is my feeling that in most cases, unless this behavior is broken, it will establish a lifelong pattern of running from any emotional confrontation or turmoil. Many times these children are crying out to be stopped, yet they run from the very thing they desire—to be unconditionally loved. One must discern if the running is motivated by the pain of rejection or simply a desire for attention. The former must be broken, overcome by overwhelming love and affirmation. Some have found that various forms of holding therapy have been helpful in promoting bonding in these cases. This type of acting out is usually testing the boundaries to see if the new parent's love is truly unconditional.

Cultural awareness issues

When adopting cross-culturally, special attention must be given to patterns of interaction. For example, my boys come from Liberia where the response to being verbally chastised or talked to is to avert the eyes. To look in the eyes of one who is in authority over you is a sign of disrespect. In our culture we will often say, "Look at me when I'm talking to you!" We may interpret the averting of the eyes as not listening to us, when in fact, just the opposite is happening. Being unaware of this dynamic may cause us to raise our voice or demand their eye contact at the risk of punishment, creating conflict within the child's emotions.

Be aware of another issue: just because your child has learned to speak English, or in some cases, your version of English, doesn't mean they understand the meanings of the words you use. We have found that to be the case with our boys. Liberia uses a form of English as the business language of the country, but many of the words we use are totally unfamiliar to them. This can create false expectations from the parent toward the child if they feel the child is disobedient when perhaps he or she just didn't understand. If you ask the child, "Do you understand?" they may answer yes, not wanting to have their language ignorance exposed. In fact, you may have to probe deeper, asking them to give the meanings of specific words in order to reveal their level of comprehension. This can occur within boundaries of our own nation as we have many different cultures here with the attendant language differences.

Each child will also be regenerated emotionally according to their different emotional make-up. One might be recharged by having "alone time" while another will be recharged by being around and interacting with others.

Hyper-stimulation can be a problem for some. During the early years, one of our sons was enrolled in a school classroom that had extremely "busy" walls. The teacher was nearly as frenetic as the wall adornments causing our son to become over stimulated. This resulted in occasional behavior problems that were caused by his inability to cope. Each child will also be regenerated emotionally according to their different emotional make-up. One might be recharged by having "alone time" while another will be recharged by being around and interacting with others. Special attention must be given to their need for internal restoration.

Stay engaged

Pay close attention to the type of schoolwork your child is being given. One of the favorite assignments in schools today is some form of "Identity Book" or stories written about the history of the child. Questions about the family of origin can be quite disconcerting. This can bring up much in the way of repressed feelings about the past. Many times there will be misbehavior at home, the roots of which are not obvious until the appropriately probative questions have been asked.

As I wrote in earlier pages, families that expect the child to completely adapt to the status quo rather than exhibiting flexibility towards the needs of the child are setting themselves up for difficulty. I cannot emphasize this enough. If you commit to the challenge of parenting an adoptive child, you MUST place their needs for adjustment above your own. You will need to be willing to adjust to them more than they may adjust to you.

I am reminded that, unlike a speedboat, it takes considerable time and space to turn a battleship around in the ocean. So it is with these children. Patience and perseverance are the order of the day as there will be times when it seems like change is not happening. The issues presented are usually more complex than expected, creating the need for discernment of the root causes of behavior. Powers of observation must be kicked into high gear if you are going to have success in caring for your child. You can do it! You can be an agent of healing. Don't give up! You will experience the rewards of healthy parenting.

Epilogue

Receiving the Spirit of adoption is a lifelong process....for all of us. We all have the baggage of a broken past that needs to be left behind. We also have access to luggage [call and purpose], through the grace of God, that can take us on a journey to wholeness. There are two fathers that vie for our hearts and attention: the father of lies and the Father of Love. God spoke these words to the children of Israel through Joshua:

> *Now therefore, fear the LORD, serve Him in sincerity and in truth, and put away the gods which your fathers served on the other side of the River and in Egypt. Serve the LORD! And if it seems evil to you to serve the LORD, choose for yourselves this day whom you will serve, whether the gods which your fathers served that were on the other side of the River, or the gods of the Amorites, in whose land you dwell. But as for me and my house, we will serve the LORD (Joshua 24:14-15).*

It is far more important knowing "whom" you believe than "what" you believe. If we choose to believe Satan and the many lies he wants to force upon us, we will be confined to the bondage and slavery of Egypt and our broken past will continue to rule over us. But, if we choose to believe the Father of Love and what He says about us, there is a promised land teeming with life and good fruit that awaits us.

There are no quick fixes. There is only faithful application of truth combined with perseverance and hope. Fathering the fatherless is a high calling that will at times both exasperate and exhilarate. There are no sure things, predetermined outcomes or guaranteed results as you pour out your life on behalf of another. There is only the satisfaction that comes with the understanding that in the end, after practicing undefiled and pure religion, we can expect to hear the Father's words ringing in our ears:

Well done, good and faithful servant; you have been faithful over a few things, I will make you ruler over many things. Enter into the joy of your Lord (Matthew 25:23).

What greater joy could there be than to know that you please the Father? What greater joy could there be than to know you have been the channel of Father's love and healing grace? Margaret and I are still in the trenches. We have children and grandchildren for whom we fight the good fight. We have good days and we have hard days but we know it is a battle worth fighting. Join with us as we take back what the enemy of our souls has tried to steal. All of us, who embrace the call to the fatherless, can have a part in the redemptive work of Jesus upon the earth, one child at a time.

Exploring the Spirit of Adoption

To contact the author
or to order additional copies of this book

Dennis L. Nice
2110 NW St. Andrews Dr.
McMinnville, OR 98128

Email dln@healingthefatherless.com
Web www.healingthefatherless.com

To order

Send $9.99 USD plus shipping and handling:
USA—$3.00 Canada—$4.00
Make checks payable to Dennis L. Nice

For quantities of the book, please contact us.

Exploring the Spirit of Adoption

MISDIRECTION

"Who knew that magic and misdirection could be applied to sales, politics, social media, and just about everything we encounter in modern life? Taylor Hughes knew, and he has written an informative and entertaining book to prove it!"

    —Lance Burton, master magician

"We've been fooled! Leave it to a magician to expose the deceptions we face every day. Wonderfully insightful, you'll be glad he's on our side."

    —Michael Jamin, television writer, producer, showrunner

"Taylor Hughes is an expert proponent of the misdirection that can be entertaining, and an insightful critic of the misdirection used to deceive us in everyday life. In this honest and conversational book, he explains how we can see through these deceptions and avoid the traps that have been set to fool us."

    —Jim Steinmeyer, author, inventor, and designer of magical illusions and theatrical special effects

"It's hard to see the picture when you are standing in the frame. Taylor's book helps us zoom out to see where we might have been misdirected and how we can find the real magic in our lives."

    —Jack Goldfinger, entertainment director for the Magic Castle, Hollywood

"When I first met Taylor Hughes, it was obvious that he was a very skilled illusionist. But as I got to know him over the years, it became clear that he was using these illusions not to bring fame to himself,

"*Misdirection* invites us to take a good look at the things that influence us the most and helps us understand why. Whether we choose to wear rose-colored glasses or not, we all benefit from living more authentic lives."

   —**Maria Goff,** author

"A great book to keep you out of trouble in this rapidly changing world. With this knowledge on your side, you'll be immune to manipulation by those after your money or worse. And now that you're such a wise, kind, and good-looking person, why not come see Piff the Magic Dragon, live in Las Vegas at the Flamingo Hotel & Casino, five nights a week, 7:00 p.m.? You owe it to yourself. Don't you?"

   —**Piff the Magic Dragon,** Las Vegas headliner

MISDIRECTION

MISDIRECTION: A Magician's Guide to Spotting and Avoiding
Manipulation in Your Life

© 2023 by Taylor Hughes

Cataloging-in-Publication data on file with the Library of Congress

ISBN: 978-1-7377073-1-8
eISBN: 978-1-7377073-2-5

Published in Upland, CA, by WonderFull Entertainment

Printed in the United States of America

MISDIRECTION

A MAGICIAN'S GUIDE TO

SPOTTING AND AVOIDING MANIPULATION IN YOUR LIFE

TAYLOR HUGHES

*Life's greatest secrets are not found in
the wisdom we have,
but in the questions we ask.*

CONTENTS

FOREWORD

We all remember that uncle or neighbor who reached in our direction when we were children and appeared to pull a nickel out of our nose or ear. *How did he do that?* We wondered and delighted in not knowing. Something inside us knew there was no coin lodged in our head, but it didn't matter to us, because we loved the possibility that *maybe, just maybe,* there was.

A good illusionist introduces us to the possibility that our assumptions may have been misplaced. In these pages you are going to hear from someone who has mastered the art of helping people consider the possibilities with truthfulness, wisdom, and wit. You are entering a master class which will help you sort out truth from deception, identify lasting things over temporal ones, and rediscover a little joy which you may have misplaced in the busyness of life.

Taylor has been a friend of mine for years. He is the best kind of storyteller because he invites us to join in every story; he makes the stories about us, not him. I have seen Taylor take the stage in front of thousands of people and hold them spellbound, and I have sat with him around a campfire with a dozen equally engaged friends. When Taylor performs, people don't feel deceived—they feel engaged. Love and truthfulness and wisdom and a childlike joy are the only things Taylor has up his sleeves in these pages. As you read his words, something will reawaken within in you, some of the fuzziness will be cut away and clarified, and the clock in your life will be reset.

It is with great delight and anticipation that I introduce to you my good friend, Taylor Hughes. Buckle up; you are going to love what you are about to experience in these pages.

—Bob Goff
author of the *New York Times* bestselling books
Everybody, Always; *Dream Big*;
Love Does; and *Undistracted*

FROM WONDER TO MISDIRECTION

I have spent a lifetime learning how to deceive people. This is possibly the greatest paradox of my life, as someone who genuinely cares for others. However, deception is part of a magician's job description. In fact, it is the primary tool magicians use to captivate and mesmerize their audiences. I must convince you that the most important thing is happening over here while the true secret to the illusion is hiding just a few feet away.

I have no problem with this level of deceit. The truth is, in the world of magic, misdirection is a beautiful thing. Audience members agree to allow themselves to be deceived when they buy a ticket to the show. We know that when the magician says there is just one ball and three cups, something else is going on that we can't see. We gladly welcome the lack of knowledge because we know we will be delighted with the outcome of the presentation.

However, misdirection in real life is rarely discussed.

Misdirection has found its way off the theatrical stage and into our businesses, politics, and even churches. In some cases, the people utilizing these techniques of distraction are unaware of the harm they are causing. However, in more scenarios than we would like to admit, the motives are much more intentional and detrimental.

So read on. When you learn to recognize misdirection, you'll see what (and who) is really calling the shots in your life, your work, and your community. It's time for us to learn the tricks of the trade so that we can help each other avoid the traps of misdirection that are being set before us daily—not to make us live in the fear of the unknown, but to discover the freedom that comes from asking the right questions. Along the way, you may even find that there are some areas where you may be misdirecting yourself.

In each chapter, we'll discuss several ways that misdirection occurs in our day-to-day activities, and afterward, I'll explain a magic trick in detail to give you a peek at the methods of misdirection. In addition, you can visit taylorhughes.com/misdirection to see videos of how they're done.

—Taylor Hughes

CHAPTER I

MISDIRECTION
IN MARKETING AND SALES

As my wife and I walked onto the car dealership lot, I leaned over and said, "We aren't buying a car today." The funny thing is, I actually believed this, not realizing that the same manipulation I use to make a living was about to be used on me with great success.

Method One: Controlling the Conversation

If you have ever visited a used car dealership, you know the mental gymnastics you can go through as you contemplate a purchase. You enter the lot with your guard up and tell yourself that you are just there to browse. In fact, that is the first thing you say when you are approached by a salesman who looks a little too calm and confident. You quickly determine by the tailoring of his suit and the wristwatch he's wearing that this guy is an expert at closing the deal, but you will not be falling for his tactics. He tells you to take all the time you want and look around.

As he heads back into the office, he asks if there is a certain model you want to look at. You tell him, and he says, "We have a few over here," then casually asks, "What is your favorite color?" You tell him you like black—and before you know it, you are sitting in the driver's seat of the exact car you just mentioned.

The whole time, you are waiting for him to say the classic used-car salesman line: "What is it going to take for you to drive this home today?" He never says it, though. He just continues asking you questions that happen to be loosely related to the car: "Do you have kids? I bet they enjoy watching movies. Did I mention this has a TV built into the back of each headrest?"

He doesn't seem to be selling you at all; he is just talking about normal stuff. You let down your guard as you take the car for a test drive.

The whole time, the salesman continues asking you seemingly unrelated things. "I noticed you have an iPhone; do you like it?" As you share why you love your phone, he mentions that this car comes equipped with Apple CarPlay. Before you know it, you are signing paperwork and driving off the lot, feeling great about the decision you made all on your own.

We all want to think that these sales tactics won't work on us—that we are impervious to the influence of others. That is why, when it does happen to us, we justify the choices we made as if we did exactly what we wanted all along. We tell our friends about that purchase like it is the greatest decision we have ever made. It almost sounds like we are trying to convince them to buy one, too, but in reality, we are trying to convince ourselves that we didn't make a mistake. My father-in-law once told me that people have to continue convincing themselves that they have made the right decision so they don't live with regret. (Very insightful—and also concerning, considering that it was coming from the man who said he approved of me marrying his daughter.)

When I was a child, I was obsessed with TV infomercials. I loved to watch those thirty-minute-long sales pitches—usually for the comedic value, but also because I found the whole structure fascinating. Infomercials are designed to make us believe that the product being advertised is the secret to unlocking our true potential as humans. As someone who loves magic and the ability to present something to skeptics in a way that will get them to believe what I am telling them, these shows were a masterclass in getting people to let down their guard. Let's look at an example of how this works.

> **TV Voiceover:** Introducing the Flaberstat 3000.
> **At-home viewer:** Here we go again. What are they trying to sell me now?
> **VO:** A revolutionary kitchen tool that will save you time, money, and stress.
> **Viewer:** How is it going to do that?
> **VO:** Just watch as Debbie loads fresh vegetables, raw meat, and grain into the Flaberstat, and in just three minutes a fully cooked meal for four is ready for your table.
> **Viewer:** What!? There is no way this thing works.

VO: I know what you're thinking. "There is no way this thing works." But don't take our word for it. Let's ask Carl.

Viewer: Carl is probably an actor.

VO: We found Carl walking down the street just moments ago.

Viewer: All right Carl, give us the truth.

Carl: Truth is, I was surprised how easy and delicious this meal was.

Viewer: That does sound pretty good, but it's probably expensive.

VO: What would you expect to pay for a machine like this?

Viewer: I don't know . . . a thousand dollars?

VO: A thousand dollars? Not today.

Viewer: How much?

VO: Today only, you get the Flaberstat 3000 for only $300.

Viewer: That isn't bad, but I don't have all that to spend now.

VO: Call today and we will split the payments into three monthly installments.

Viewer: Oh, that's great, but it's still just a little too expensive.

VO: Call in the next ten minutes and we will knock off one of the payments.

Viewer: This is too good to pass up, but I am supposed to use this money to buy a present for my mom's birthday.

VO: Act now and we will also send you this free underwater flashlight that also makes popcorn.
Viewer: Mom will love that! DONE.

Years ago, businesses were usually focused on creating products they thought we would want and then convincing us how great they were. Now, thanks to target marketing and the ability to see what we are searching for on the internet—which is also a way of controlling the conversation—there is very little guesswork involved on their part. Companies don't have to wonder if you want tie-dyed knee-high socks; they *know* because you searched for them online moments ago. And we've likely all experienced a moment when we found the perfect item online and think, *I would love to have that but it's too much*. So we go to Facebook, and suddenly there is an ad with a promo code for people in your zip code. What a coincidence! Right?

It isn't magic; it's marketing.

Some people honestly want to stay off the grid and not let anyone know what they are doing, but the truth is, anyone with the right software already knows what you are doing. If you have a phone on your person and you enter a business, a digital perimeter can be drawn around that building that shows the IP address of every device that enters it during operating hours. Interested parties can then track where those devices go at the end of the day, within a few houses. That business now knows where their customers are coming from, what neighborhood they live in, etc.

A few years ago, companies had to send out surveys to understand who their customers were. Now, this data is readily available. Thanks to algorithms, online shopping is even more targeted. You know when you are shopping online, and the site says "people who bought this item also were interested in these items"? As a consumer, we tend to think that information is there to help us find what we are looking for, but from a business standpoint, being able to track your client's search history and know what they bought and what other items they might be interested in is invaluable.

It's helpful to remember that strangers know more about you than you think. Spam email scams are often based on having one small piece of information about you. If I know that you bought something at a store, I can text or email you while pretending to be that store and say your payment didn't go through and I need your credit card information to make sure it does.

In both the used-car and infomercial scenarios above, the salesmen make a point of asking questions like "Isn't this a great deal?" or "Wouldn't you enjoy driving a car like this?" to create the illusion that you have thought through the decision, but the questions are meant to push you toward his desired outcome. In both situations, you would benefit by asking some other questions, like "Is this the best way to spend my money?" or "Will this purchase add value to my life or create more stress?"

The antidote to misdirection is always to ask more questions.

Method Two: Selling an Easy Fix

It can be easy to believe that someone else knows what's best, and if you just follow these simple steps, join that program, or buy their product, your life will be better. One-stop-shop solutions are attractive because they appear to save us time, money, or effort—but some of life's biggest problems don't have simple answers. Paying someone who says they will achieve your goals for you might seem like a good idea, but often these deals are full of empty promises and false advertisements. Our desire to have it all without having to do it all makes us susceptible to these types of scams.

There is a game in Las Vegas that isn't played on the casino floor, but rather on the sidewalk out front. It consists of a makeshift table—usually an upside-down trash can or cardboard box—between the person playing the "game" and the passersby hoping to win. This procedure goes by different names, such as Find the Lady, the Three-Card Monte, and the Old Shell Game. The game pieces vary from playing cards to walnut shells; sometimes three upside-down cups and a ball are employed. All you need to know, though, is that this is a game you can't win. Even calling it a "game" is misleading; this is a con. The person throwing the cards or mixing the cups is a skilled sleight-of-hand artist, and every word, movement, and nuance has been carefully choreographed to ensure you leave without your money.

How do you recognize one of these "games"? The first thing you see is a crowd gathered around one person who is explaining the rules. "It's a simple game of chance. In fact, you can hardly lose. Just guess which one of these cups I place the ball under as I mix them up. You are guaranteed to be correct at least a third of the time."

You watch as someone approaches the man; he bets twenty dollars and correctly guesses which cup the ball is under. The person mixing the cups says, "Double or nothing." The player takes the bet and wins! The dealer congratulates him as he leaves with his winnings and disappears down the street. You think, *Well, this looks like fun.* You observe another game and see someone lose, but you are certain if they had chosen the cup you were thinking of, they would have won. So you step up to the plate, already planning what you will do with your winnings.

You bet big and lose it all. How is this possible?

The reality is the dealer is a magician who has never lost the game. He is so skilled in the invisible acrobatics required to make the ball move effortlessly from one cup to another that you will never see the moment when he takes advantage of you.

If that is the case though, what about the person you just watched win big? Well, he is in on it. The technical name for that role is "the shill," and that person is the dealer's secret partner. They will meet up later to divide the winnings.

I have spent countless hours studying this game. It is a beautiful symphony of deceit. The irony is, most of the time the loser walks away having had a great time and not realizing he has been conned.

It is easy to feel bad for those who have been scammed this way, to feel they have been victimized by a cruel game. However, the individual's desire to get rich quickly is what leads them down the path of misdirection.

Because we want to believe it is possible to win this low-risk, high-reward game, we overlook many things that should have caused us to pause before playing. If the dealer was repeatedly losing, why would he keep offering to play? If it is possible to win big, why have we never heard those stories? (You can, however, recall stories of someone betting it all and losing.) Our own greed clouds our vision. We need to ask ourselves some tough questions about our intentions.

Just as there is a name for the shill who helps build the illusion, there is one used to describe the person being conned: the mark.

Professional con artists spend a great deal of time determining who will most likely fall for their schemes. The game doesn't work on everyone, so you want to find a mark who will be an easy target. The best mark is one who is so focused on what's in it for them that they make poor decisions along the way—a guy trying to impress his girlfriend, a casino patron who wants to win back what she just lost, or the boss who wants to show his employees at the convention how smart he is. Our pride, greed, and ego tend to lead us into these types of traps.

I have presented versions of this game on stage many times, and I can tell you that success is based loosely on the sleight of hand skills, but mostly on choosing the right mark. Stealing a volunteer's watch has been a staple in my shows for years. It is a skill that takes an insane amount of practice and guts to pull off (get it??? Pull off?). I always return pickpocketed goods, and because I am not collecting items to sell, I don't go for the most expensive or difficult watches to steal. While I have learned different techniques to acquire any type of watch, some are easier to get off than others. Therefore, I generally go for watches that are easier to remove. Why would I work harder than I need to? This is also true of real con artists. They are looking for easy marks because the quicker they can take advantage of you, the sooner they move on to the next victim.

Your goal should be to become a terrible mark. This starts with asking the right questions.

Method Three: Rushing the Decision

One way to recognize manipulation in your everyday life is to look for situations in which you are being pressured to make quick decisions. Most buyer's remorse comes from decisions we didn't have the time to think through. A limited-time offer that sounds too good to be true often is. Most of us would never buy chewing gum or tabloid magazines if they weren't at the register; if there were a tabloid section at the grocery store, you would probably pass it every time because that's not why you went there. The time in which you have to decide if you want that Kit-Kat bar is compressed because the cashier and other customers are waiting. There is an entire industry built around these types of impulse items.

In performance art, whether comedy or magic, the surprise is often achieved by timing. In a joke, the time between the set-up and the punchline is called compression. Expert joke writers understand the importance of tightening this gap. The more compressed a joke is, the more surprised the audience will be and the bigger the laugh will be. This means the fewer words you can use to get the point across, the better. In a magic show, compression is useful when a borrowed item vanishes and then appears in a different place. The shorter the time from when the object vanishes to its reappearance, the more impressive and impossible the illusion seems to the audience.

This same technique is used in sales and marketing. The phrase "time is money" encourages salespeople to move fast when closing deals. Bonuses are given based on how much is accomplished in a given period of time. The quicker you get to the finish line, the greater the reward. This means that often, the pressure faced by sales team members is passed on to their clients.

Limited-time offers and scarcity are often used to rush you to a decision without allowing time to ask important questions. If you feel you are being rushed toward a decision, this is a good time to slow down and ask more questions. In some cases, stepping away from the situation momentarily will give you a chance to examine all the options with a clear head.

Method Four: False Advertising and Empty Promises

Another classic con goes by the name "Jam Auction." In the United Kingdom, this is called a *run out* (since most people who present this con will be run out of town). The person running the "auction" begins by drawing a crowd by saying they are giving away lots of amazing items. Often, this is done in the back of a box truck that appears to be packed with expensive items like cell phones and televisions. The con operator says they have enough items for everyone who gets one of these bags, but you must have a bag to win. Once the bags are passed out to the crowd, the people who a few moments earlier were planning to walk away are locked in. After all, they have received a bag and want to stick around to see what they will win.

The first item is usually a small trinket, like a pen set available at any dollar store. The con artists describe it as if it normally sells for thirty dollars, "but who would pay one dollar for it today?" and then ask to see your dollar. The salesman or attendant takes the money from everyone who holds up a dollar and hands them the pen, which they put in the bag. The con artist may even have the participants yell a catchphrase—like, "When I say, 'Is it good?' you say, 'It's all good!'" Everyone who complies gets their money back. The con artist repeats this process with increasingly impressive items, slowly increasing the amount the customers pay—but every time, after saying the catchphrase, they return the money, leaving the spectators pleased with all the free stuff they are getting.

The heist concludes with a high-priced item like a watch, also secretly purchased from a dollar store. After getting everyone to pay up fifty dollars for the watch, the con artist repeats the catchphrase. But this time, when the audience says, "It's all good!" the con men close the truck's roll-up door and drive away. Everyone in the audience is left holding a bag of things they didn't want that's worth about five dollars, when they paid fifty.

The psychology behind this—overpromising and underdelivering—is similar to many modern-day marketing techniques. Have you ever seen a commercial for a new hamburger that you just *had* to try, only to get the actual thing and find that it looked *nothing* like what you saw in the commercial? We can easily get caught up in the excitement of advertisements and marketing campaigns, but if we learn to slow down and ask some questions, it is possible to spot misdirection and run it out of town.

Next time you're out shopping, whether in-person or online, slow down. Take a breath. Reflect before you act.

On the next page are some questions to ask when you're facing a purchasing decision. Better yet, ask these questions with your family or a group of friends. Together, you can demystify the misdirection we all commonly face.

As with most types of misdirection, we need to look past the information being presented to us and ask some different questions. Every day, we make choices and too often assume that no one has influenced our decisions. Everything from the shampoo we buy to the clothing we pick out at the store has been influenced through marketing. As you go about your day, take notice of how many influential ads you can count before it becomes overwhelming.

Remember that this exposure is happening constantly, and it is having an impact whether you realize it or not.

QUESTIONS TO ASK IN A SALES SITUATION

1. What problem am I trying to solve? Will this purchase address that issue? Will it create other issues?
2. Is this fulfilling a need or just a desire?
3. Have I taken adequate time to consider this decision?
4. Who do I know that would have a good perspective on this situation? Can I ask that person for advice?
5. By making this purchase, what am I saying yes to? What will I need to say no to as a result?

Behind the Curtain #1

PICK A CARD

Here is a simple but effective magic trick that utilizes the principles we just discussed to create a delightful illusion. It is probably the first trick you think of when you see a magician holding a deck of cards, and it is a perfect example of how rushing a decision can lead to misdirection.

The Trick

The magician shows you an ordinary deck of cards and even allows you to shuffle them. Once you confirm that the deck is normal in every way, the performer spreads it out and asks you to pick a card, any card. You make your selection, and the magician instantly knows what it is.

The Secret

There are many ways to achieve this effect, but for the purposes of our discussion, let's use the one called the classic force. This can be accomplished with a standard deck of playing cards, and while it takes a lot of practice, it is one of the best skills magicians can keep in their bag of tricks.

As the performer, you spread the cards, allowing the participant to choose any one, but time it in such a way that he is forced to select the card of your choosing. This is done by first knowing the identity of the bottom card of the pack. The cards have previously been shuffled, and the bottom card can be glimpsed as you square up the deck.

When you are ready to force a card, you will do the following moves:

- Cut the cards with your right hand, bringing the bottom half over the top half in your left hand (see video link on the next page for further reference.)
- Before placing the cards together, place the pad of your left pinky finger on top of the back right corner of the lowest packet of cards. Your pinky will stay in this position, holding what is known as a pinky break. You are left with the card face-down in your left hand.
- The spectators will see an ordinary stack of cards. However, your pinky finger retains a break above the card you glimpsed earlier. Let's say it's the five of hearts.
- You now begin to spread the cards from the top of the pack in your left hand and over to your right, allowing

your participant to see the backs of the cards as they decide where to stop you.

- You will need to time your spread of the cards to the point of the break as the participant reaches for a card.

This takes a lot of practice, but once you master it, you will be able to make your participant feel he had a free choice when in fact you have forced him to select that card you chose.

To see a video breaking down how this trick is performed, visit **taylorhughes.com/misdirection.**

CHAPTER 2

MISDIRECTION IN THE NEWS

My first crush was not the girl next door or a classmate at school, but a fictional surfer I saw on a TV show called *Gidget*. Sure, she was a few years older than me, but I was sure she would've waited for me to grow up. I told my mom about my love for Gidget, since she would be spending a lot of time with her soon.

My mom shattered my dream by telling me that *Gidget* was a rerun that had first aired more than twenty-five years earlier. I was devastated by the realization that my crush was already grown up with a family of her own and would soon be acting in commercials for bone health products.

That's how I learned it's a critical mistake to assume that everything I saw on TV was actually happening—even the news.

Method One: If It Bleeds, It Leads

Reporting the news is a public service, but it is also a business. As we will see over and over, the desire for money is often the root of misdirection. The media, regardless of type, makes money from viewership. Programming is designed to entice you to watch, keep your attention, and build loyalty. Like any business, news outlets are run by individuals with specific perspectives and biases. While we would hope that journalists and news organizations recognize their responsibility to report the facts objectively, we need to take responsibility as consumers and ask more questions.

Years ago, the input we received from the media was mostly the same for all of us. There were only a handful of TV channels, and the news was not on twenty-four seven. In fact, every station went dark at midnight. Limited programming ensured that the next day, everyone would be talking about who was on *The Ed Sullivan Show* or that episode of *Jackie Gleason* that made them laugh. The news was just the news; it didn't necessarily lean one way or the other. Reporters would just give the facts that were available about the events that had occurred.

But as more content was created and audiences grew, TV executives discovered they could monetize television by selling program sponsorships and eventually ad space, and the programs got longer. After all, the longer you stayed tuned in, the more commercials could be sold and the more money there was to be made.

Anchors began teasing content going into commercial breaks in order to get audiences to stick around. They even began encouraging viewers to tune in to the nightly news by creating their own commercials, asking questions like, "Is your drinking water safe?

Find out tonight at 8 p.m." Viewers would go thirsty the rest of the day as they waited to find out the answer.

When evaluating a particular news source, a good question to ask is, "Who will benefit from me watching this?" If the programming affects you emotionally—making you angry, happy, or fearful—you are more likely to stay glued to the TV, which translates to more money and higher ratings for someone else.

The desire to protect our families, our homes, and our way of life is a natural human instinct. This is why we can scroll past stories about heartbreaking events on the other side of the globe and feel little concern while panicking about soaring gas prices at home. Rightly or wrongly, our survival instinct causes us to want to look out for ourselves more than others. It is important to realize that the media understand this as well. Sources who desire to manipulate, misdirect, or motivate us to act in their interest will often use the fear of loss to keep us tuned in. If you find that your main sources of news tend to be fear-driven, misdirection may be involved.

Method Two: Too Much to Take In

Every day we are inundated with information. In addition to whatever you woke up thinking about today, you are constantly being bombarded with other people's thoughts, opinions, and expectations. From the minute you wake up, advertisers are vying for your attention. It is estimated that the average person is exposed to four thousand to ten thousand advertisements a day.[1] This can be overwhelming, and yet it's hard to avoid because we need to stay informed about what's going on in the world.

So we find ways to streamline our news consumption. Instead of watching a two-hour televised town hall, we watch three-minute recaps or look for a YouTuber who can summarize the highlights, thinking, *Just tell me what I need to know so I can get on with my day*. Since these programs by their very nature have to edit out most of the actual events, it is important to look for any bias in your sources. Outlets can easily exclude facts that might be inconvenient for their agendas. Knowing you are too busy to check their work, they just omit information that might sway your opinion. It is no mistake that headlines go on the front page of a newspaper, and retractions, if needed, are often buried in the small print several pages in.

Another downside of this constant flow of information is fatigue. It is not unusual to hear people discussing an issue that has been widely reported say, "I'm just tired. I can't watch it anymore." This happens often during election cycles, when being informed is paramount. When things get overwhelming, it is easy to start checking out. However, we cannot blame others if we are uninformed. So how do we sort through this overwhelming amount of information and make good decisions?

I have a dear friend who lives in the United Kingdom. We often have long chats about the differences and similarities between the places we live. I am amazed that Brits can go to the doctor without paying a dime, and he is mostly amazed that we have the Cheesecake Factory.

The Cheesecake Factory taught me how to make better decisions. Its incredibly large menu is both exciting and daunting. It feels like you have to do a collegiate research project before the meal comes. Also, there are no pictures, which I relied on to choose my meals at every restaurant I visited before I was twenty. When I started going to nicer restaurants, though, the pictures went away. To combat this, I created a workaround that I still use to this day: I walk around the restaurant to check out what everyone else is eating. I make mental notes of what looks good, then come back and let the server know I will have the spinach dip and whatever is on that flaming plate at table fourteen.

We can use this same approach to how we take in news. Rather than just taking someone else's recommendation, what if we looked at several sources? What if we got several perspectives and then made our decisions based on all the information available to us?

It is possible to develop "trusted sources"—journalists, thought leaders from various areas of expertise, some podcasters, even friends whose insights you have learned to trust. Additionally, there are media watchdogs (in other words, people who report on reporters) who rate news sources according to certain criteria. One of these is Ad Fontes Media Bias, which rates news and news-like sources on a chart by how biased (or unbiased) they are, where they fall on the mix of fact and analysis, whether they engage in propaganda, and so on. You can also engage with many of these outlets through their websites and social media, and ask questions that will help you find resources you can trust.

Method Three: Fake News

Often after a magic show, people want to tell the performer how they think the trick worked. This is my favorite time of the night. Sometimes people present methods to me that have never crossed my mind, throwing around elaborate ideas about systems of pullies and wires, magnets and mirrors. The funniest is when someone just shouts, "Fake, it's all fake!" This makes me laugh because I say very clearly in every presentation that I don't claim to have any special powers—this is all just for fun.

Over the last several years this kind of attitude has popped up in arguments over the news media, led by government officials at the highest levels. It's important to remember that the Founding Fathers felt that a free press was so important that they enshrined it in the First Amendment to the U.S. Constitution.

If we are not diligent to fact-check the news we see—regardless of which station reports it—we run the risk of passing the baton of misinformation on to others. How often has a friend or family member shared some news with you and used the phrase "They say that . . ."? The first question we should ask is, "Who are *they*?" We tend to use the word "they" as a catch-all, but the answer to that question is both specific and crucial.

Once you know who said something, you can ask the next question: "Why did they say that?" Is it because that is factually what happened, or does the source have an ulterior motive for wanting us to be misinformed?

We now have resources at our disposal that were not available in the past. If you want to know what really happened, in almost any case, you can find out. It is our responsibility, though, to do the research required.

Some people will claim they have the freedom to believe whatever they want, but this is a dangerous position to take. In our judicial system, rulings are made based on the facts we know. If you have ever been on a jury, you know that your responsibility is to weigh the evidence of the case and make a decision based on the facts that have been presented, not on your personal bias or opinion. This is to ensure a fair trial and outcome for all involved. However, the court of public opinion is being negatively influenced by the idea that one can simply choose to ignore facts that don't fit a particular agenda. While you have the right to an opinion, you need to be able to defend that opinion with facts.

If you find yourself questioning the truth of something in the news, find a fact-checking organization you believe you can trust—but keep in mind that these are not free of biases or agendas either, so it's worthwhile to find out who funds it (or which causes it funds) to see if those values line up with your own. "Follow the money" is always the best way to find out who is pulling the strings.

Actual fake news or misinformation occurs when unconfirmed opinions are presented as fact and actual true events are ignored. This is why it is important to continue asking questions and to always fact-check information when it is reported. An interesting experiment to conduct the next time a big news event occurs is to watch several different sources' reports. Watch a presidential debate so you know what is actually said, and then watch two or three different outlets' coverage. You will begin to see the angles and biases that sneak in as anchors and guests translate what they think happened in real time.

Method Four: Tell Them What They Want to Hear

Confirmation bias is probably the most important aspect to be aware of when considering misdirection in the news. It is very easy to misdirect yourself by seeking out media that will tell you only what you want to hear. There is only so much news to share each day, and therefore, reporting has become only a small part of the news day. The rest is padded with reactions, interviews, recaps, and theories about what might happen next. News anchors have become celebrities because people like their take on things, and now they have their own shows through which to present the news that is important to them. As the internet has grown more popular, everyday citizens have begun creating their own platforms through which to share their personal takes on everything from voting laws to which brand of coffee is best.

Thanks to marketing trends (see Chapter 1), news programming now targets opinions and groups. As a result, we are able to tune into programs that confirm our biases. In turn, those programs keep producing popular content in order to keep us tuned in during commercial breaks. This happens so often that we can now curate content that only tells us what we already want to hear, and we call it the news.

How do we recognize when we're doing this? One way is to look at the types of products being sold through space on your news station. If you watch programming that talks constantly about the volatility of the stock market and then see ads for buying gold, take notice. If you watch an hour-long segment about struggling farmers and the show is sponsored by a fair-trade coffee company, take notice.

When I was a kid in the 1980s, my elementary school library contained a set of research encyclopedias. When we wanted to learn about a subject or needed to write a school report, we would go to the encyclopedia and find information about that topic. It became hard to make our work stand out from everyone else's because we were all using the same source material. But now, we must remember that when we go online, we are not seeing the same things everyone else is seeing. We are seeing a version of the world that has been curated to fit our likes, prejudices, and opinions. Knowing that this is how the internet works, it is helpful to ask questions and look outside your current information sources when trying to make informed decisions.

Psychics have built empires around telling people what they want to hear. The best way for a psychic to impress someone is to have intimate details about that person. Some mediums will have you write down a question or situation you want to know about—and then secretly peek at it. If you have made an appointment online with a psychic, remember it is quite easy for them to find your social media accounts to find out details about you that you have forgotten the whole world can see, and then say things like, "I know you recently traveled somewhere exotic." "I'm seeing a man who always wears a blue hat." "You recently experienced a loss."

In the past, these "mind readers" needed to find unique ways to create psychic connections with total strangers. One of the oldest methods, still used to this day, is called "cold reading." This involves looking at things like a person's body language, clothing, speech cadence, etc., to find out personal details. Is she wearing a wedding ring? Does his clothing mention a place he may have visited or gone to college? Any religious jewelry?

While we don't want to make assumptions or snap judgments about people, this is one of the primary tactics used by psychics. Sometimes they will throw out incredibly vague information, yet the participant will help them by either filling in the blanks or claiming that these generic descriptions are spot on. (Psychologists refer to this as the "Forer Effect"— after researcher Bertram Forer. But it also is sometimes called the "Barnum Effect" since it was heavily utilized by showman P. T. Barnum.) Here is an example of how this could look in a group setting:

Medium: I'm getting the sense that someone here is really upset with someone who is not here. Perhaps there was a fight. I don't know if this is a romantic relationship or a family relationship, but it's someone very close to you, and you feel uneasy about where things stand between you and this person. I am seeing the letter S. I'm not sure if that makes sense to anyone. Maybe their name begins with S.

(A member of the audience raises a hand).

Medium: Yes, I believe it is you. Does that mean anything to you at all?

Volunteer: Yes, that's definitely me.

Medium: Can you share with us a little about the altercation you had with this person?

Volunteer: Yes, it's my coworker, Jerry. We share a cubicle.

Medium: Yes, I felt that this was someone who was close to you, that you spend a lot of time with him.

Volunteer: Earlier today we got in a fight because he ate my lunch, and I'm not looking forward to going to work tomorrow.

Medium: Yes, that uneasiness I was sensing. Who is "S"?

Volunteer: Serena is my supervisor.

Medium: So, you get along with Serena?

Volunteer: Yes, she is incredible.
Medium: I just get this urge that you need to confide in Serena, and this situation with Jerry will resolve itself.

In this scenario, the volunteer credited the psychic for knowing all this information about her, when in fact the psychic didn't know what she was going to say until the volunteer spoke. The participant so badly wanted to experience this moment that she made the connection for the medium. This confirmation bias causes the person desiring the results to give credit where it is not due. In the same way, people seek out news that will confirm their existing biases.

Method Five: Prioritizing Profit

As we have seen earlier, money often lies at the root of manipulation. The news is big business, and viewership translates to profit margin. Programmers are rewarded for increasing audience size and attention. Stories can be prioritized based not on importance, but on what will get the most clicks or views.

Asking questions about what isn't being reported will help keep you safe. It is a mistake to assume that if a detail or event is important, you will hear about it on the evening news. News programs are curated, and part of that process means being selective about what is shared. There may be other stories and updates that are still important, but not as profitable for the outlets to report. Reminding yourself of this also will keep you from being discouraged by only seeing negative things on the news. The world is full of amazing stories of people caring for one another. Those just don't get featured as much because unfortunately, negativity gets noticed.

Most news sites carry advertisements on their pages. Many of these sites have gone so far as to design these ads to look like the new stories you are there to read. What appears to be an article about mortgage rates is actually an advertisement for a mortgage lender who wants to refinance your house. It is good to stay vigilant and ask more questions about the news sources you consume. Remember that if it can get your attention, it can be monetized.

Sometimes the way things become news may surprise you. Here is an example: Your favorite news anchor opens a segment by letting you know that this year, spider infestations have increased. He then adds some facts about how the type of weather we have been experiencing leads to increased spider activity. He then brings on an expert guest to share what we can do to protect our homes: Ray from Ray's Pest Service.

If you are watching this passively, you may think the news channel became aware of the spider problem and designed this segment to help us all out. In reality, Ray was looking for ways to get the word out about his business, and he created a press release that shared info about spiders and offered to go on the news to talk about it. A segment producer realized she could make this into a story if she sensationalized it a little, and now you are convinced that spiders will soon lay siege to your house if you don't act fast.

A good question to ask as you are watching the news is: What is the story *behind* the story? You see a news segment about the Fourth of July that features the history of apple pie and its American roots. The anchors have even brought in Flo from the local bakery to show you how to make an apple pie; at the end of the segment, you find out that if you're too busy to make your own, you can just stop by Flo's to place your order. What is the story behind the story?

My wife's grandfather was a news videographer in the 1960s. He told us about the time he was asked to film a union strike happening downtown. By the time he arrived, the picketers had gone home for the evening. Another news station's team arrived at the same time and decided to get people hanging out downtown to act as thought they were picketing. And these types of things continue to happen across all media today.

Remember there's always more than one way to tell—or create—a story.

Learning about all the ways misdirection works against us can be a little disheartening. It becomes so obvious once we are informed of these tactics that we can feel foolish for not knowing before. But we can't be expected to know everything; how could we? Around five hundred hours of new content are uploaded to YouTube each minute.[2] To watch only what is currently on the platform would take you approximately eighteen thousand years! We have access to more information than ever before and could never consume all that is available. However, when someone is conned, his first thought is that he should have known better. Let's put the judgment aside and shift that to say "we *could* have known." While there are some incredibly beautiful mysteries in life that we cannot fathom, we can learn and grow in our knowledge of almost any subject by asking more questions.

QUESTIONS TO ASK WHEN WATCHING THE NEWS

1. Who is making money from the media I am consuming?
2. What is my current relationship with confirmation bias?
3. What do my trusted news sources say about this?
4. Have I researched anything new this week? Why or why not?
5. Which do I value more—being right or knowing the truth?
6. When was the last time I changed my mind about an important issue?
7. What is the story behind the story?

DUAL REALITY

One of the greatest tools a magician can use is called dual reality. In this, he creates a scenario in which separate parts of the audience see different things but assume that everyone saw the same thing. Here is an example of dual reality at work in the form of an illusion: The participant assumes that the card he is signing is the one the audience sees, and the audience assumes that the signature they are looking at belongs to your onstage participant. But they are all wrong.

The Trick

The performer brings a volunteer on stage and has that person select a card from a deck. (Let's say it's the three of spades.) The participant signs it with a permanent marker, and the magician then shows this card to the audience. Everyone watches as he burns the signed card with a lighter. The ashes float up, and the performer catches the last piece of ash on top of the deck. He then lifts the card off the top of the deck, showing the audience the signed card they all think he just burned to ash. The participant on stage verifies that yes, that is, in fact, the card he signed.

The Secret

To perform this trick, you will need a deck of cards and two extra three of spades cards from identical decks. Before you take the stage, sign the two duplicate cards with a fake but matching signature. Don't sign your own name, and make sure a specific name isn't legible. These will be the cards the audience sees. Place them on top of the deck.

Next, place the third three of spades on top of the deck. At this point, you should have a normal deck of cards with two duplicate signed cards on top and a third, matching card with no signature on top of these.

Invite an audience member onto the stage, and cut the top card to the center of the deck using the classic force we described earlier to make sure he selects it when you tell him to "pick any card." Have the participant sign it. As you shake the ink dry, switch this card for one on the top that you signed earlier. This technique is called the top change.

At this moment, your volunteer is seeing the back of a card he thinks he signed, but it is one of the two you signed earlier. His card is on top of the deck, and just below that is your second card with a fake signature. Set the deck down briefly and destroy the card you showed the audience (one of the ones with the fake signature) in any way you see fit, such as running it through a paper shredder, setting it on fire, or even just tearing it into tiny pieces and tossing them away. Make a magical gesture, pick up the deck, and lift the top two cards as one to show the audience the card you signed. They will be in awe because they have no idea what your participant's signature actually looks like.

Meanwhile, as you turn toward the volunteer to "verify" that the signature is his, you momentarily contact the top of the deck with the double stack of cards, and only remove the top card. This is the card he actually signed, which he can now keep as a souvenir.

To see a video breaking down how this trick is performed, visit **taylorhughes.com/misdirection.**

CHAPTER 3

MISDIRECTION
IN SOCIAL MEDIA

In the early 2000s, a new way for people to connect with each other appeared on the internet: social media. For the first time in history, you could share conversations, photos, and even videos with friends around the globe in real time. By 2004, MySpace had reached one million monthly users, and social networking was on the rise, but within a few years, it would be fully eclipsed by sites like Facebook and Instagram.[1]

The ability to build relationships through the internet has changed the world, but wherever people gather, misdirection tends to crash the party. In this section, we will look at some of the ways that misdirection is reshaping social media and what we can do to stay focused on connection.

Method One: Illusion of Connection

While people sometimes do misdirect others on social media, this is one of the areas where we mostly tend to misdirect ourselves. Many people launch social media accounts thinking they will be able to share life moments with friends and possibly make some new friends along the way. After all, that is the promise, right? Connecting to each other no matter where we are in the world?

What tends to happen, though, as you connect with more people online is that your news feed becomes another source of nonstop content. It can become hard to stay connected as we shift from engaging with others to scrolling for updates. Most of our closest relationships are the result of direct contact. Uninterrupted conversations with coworkers or neighbors allow us to get to know one another and dive below the surface-level interactions we have with most people.

On social media sites, however, due to the high volume of content being uploaded and algorithms working hard to predict what you want, you can't possibly see everything your friends post. In lieu of one-on-one conversations, social media posts are based on broadcasting messages to anyone who follows you. Therefore, your feed is populated by the posts that are getting the most attention. It is no longer just a place for friends to connect; it is a mixture of people you know, popular videos from strangers, and curated advertisements designed to capture your attention. Some companies even use Facebook as their sole avenue of advertisement—becoming yet another way to pull us away from genuine connection to distraction.

Conversely, the need to connect has sometimes been exploited by behind-the-scenes groups who manipulate both information and opinion. We know, for example, that there are groups of tweeting bots (controlled by just one person) that make observers think there is greater support or opposition for an issue than there actually is.[2] It has been reported that entire networks of fake Facebook accounts were set up in Russia that then joined Facebook groups and spouted propaganda to manipulate others' opinions.[3] And while it's nearly impossible for the average user to ferret out the truth about these networks themselves, we can do our due diligence by questioning them, researching them, and reporting them.

The way we develop relationships is through shared experiences, getting to know one another, and discussing our passions and dreams. The illusion of connection becomes strong when we and others share about our lives online. We know all about our online friends' lives. We know their favorite foods, what they thought about the movie they saw last night, who they are dating, all the things they love and hate... but we do not really know *them*. We feel connected, but we are observers. The closest thing we have to interaction is likes, shares, and comments. The same can happen with online celebrity interactions or sports teams. It is possible to feel closely connected to people who aren't aware of your existence.

Not only are we not connecting the way we want to online, but our constant need to check in virtually affects the way we interact with others in person. We have conditioned ourselves to stare at our phones whenever there is a moment of unfilled time. Couples sit next to each other on the couch with their phones in hand, sending each other videos instead of talking. Our intentions are good, but the methods we are using to build connections may actually be preventing us from living in the present. Instead of going out for coffee with a friend to catch up, we simply scroll through their feed to feel as though we are still connected. If we aren't careful, we will become spectators in other people's lives rather than living our own. Perhaps we should take a breather?

What if you took a moment right now to message someone you have been needing to connect with? Set up a lunch appointment or offer to meet them for coffee. Another good practice is to look for opportunities to connect online in ways you haven't before. If you tend to just scroll and observe, maybe you could message someone directly the next time you think about them. What would happen if the next time you were tempted to pick up the phone and check what a friend has been up to online, you just called them instead? The antidote to false connection is genuine interaction. Look for opportunities to trade the illusion for the real deal.

Method Two: Selling Perfection

As we have become an audience to the lives of others on social media, we cannot help but compare our daily experiences to theirs. It is important to remember that people tend to share mostly the highlights—their happy and successful moments. As a result, it can seem as though everyone else is perfect and your life is a mess. But remember that there are always two versions of the family vacation: the one parents post about online, and the one the children survived.

The highlight-reel factor conditions us to believe that if we share more positive things, we will be rewarded with interaction. Our desire to be noticed can lead us to paint an inaccurate picture of our lives. We assume everyone is doing better than we are because they can afford things we can't. One person will post that she is getting married, which makes someone else feel like she will never find love. The comparison game is a huge trap that misdirects us and robs us of joy.

Influencers who are famous for no reason other than having followers sell us on their version of an ideal life. *If you just look like this* (go to this link for this cute outfit), *live in this type of house with accessories you can get from this website, or find that perfect soulmate, everything will be perfect, just like you see on my Insta.* As a result, we strive for perfection as if it is a fixed goal and not an ever-moving target. Young people grow up feeling "less than" due to constant comparison. What diet and exercise don't fix, we will make up for with photoshop and filters. We post our perfectly edited pictures that others will view as reality, and one domino of manipulation hits the next.

Unhappiness rises because we can't live up to the illusion we have created. We become further isolated from each other as we spend less time with one another and more time acting as our own PR agents. This pace is exhausting.

As an entertainer, there is something great about being able to get on stage, perform for an hour, and then go back to my normal life. Many of my friends are fellow performers who work on cruise ships, and one of the challenges of doing that type of show is that you are living with the audience; you have to be "on" all the time. A similar thing is beginning to happen to all of us because of social media: We are constantly performing for one another. We've stopped seeking out experiences for pure joy and, instead, only show up so we have a photo of the event to post. This is not sustainable and will rob us of the unique and fulfilling lives we could have if we allow it.

It is dangerous to never feel like you can be honest or open. To have real relationships, we must find a group of people with whom we can be real—with whom it is safe not only to celebrate our victories but to share our struggles. We should not only be looking for friends like this, but we should seek to be this type of friend to others. What if we valued authenticity over perfection? What if we not only saw through facades that others have built, but also stopped creating our own?

Method Three: May I Have Your Attention, Please?

When I was a kid, my dad was part of a local billiards league. On Saturdays, he would play in pool tournaments, and often I got to tag along. One day, a professional trick shot artist who also performed magic came to play. I watched in amazement as he presented a series of impossible-seeming shots and tricks. Afterward, my dad told him that I also performed magic. That day, not only did the pro teach me a few new tricks, but he shared with me an important life lesson: He told me that if I got the chance to perform for people, I'd better make it worth their time. In other words: If you are going to pick up a microphone, you'd better have something to say.

With any performance, the audience is secondary to the creation of the art. Before a band books a gig, they will write and practice their music. Before a painter plans an exhibit, she will go to her studio and paint. Speakers find an audience because they have something important to share. However, social media has created a strange scenario in which having an audience is the main goal, and the creation comes less from passion and more from what will get attention.

One of the great things social media has done for creators is provide platforms that can be accessed without gatekeepers. If you had a garage band in the 1990s and wanted to record an album, you would need to spend thousands of dollars to book studio time, hire an engineer, and pay for the production costs to bring your music to the world. If you were a stand-up comedian in the 1980s and wanted to share your talent with the world, you would have to trek to open-mic events every night and hone your craft to eventually get a showcase or an audition and meet an agent that could open the door for you to find work. But musicians no longer need record labels to get airtime; they can simply upload their music to their own accounts to reach fans. Comedians are gaining followings because they are posting jokes, and audiences are finding them. Sure, lots of folks dream of getting a big break by landing on a TV show, but many of them make their own break these days. If you have something you want to share with the world, you are just a few clicks away from making that happen.

The challenge comes when we want to have an audience for no reason. After all, the only thing better than watching online celebrities is becoming one yourself. Thus, we have all become performers, broadcasting everything from what we had for lunch to our political opinions. We judge ourselves and each other based on likes and shares rather than the content of our character.

We will do whatever it takes to get attention because we feel like that will make us valuable. Our happiness is not based on the lives we live, but rather on how people react to us. If our focus becomes finding approval outside of ourselves, the misdirection has already begun. Creativity will suffer as we look to algorithms to tell us what is worth creating. Artists stop producing what is in their hearts and instead create what they know will get shared. We see fewer stories of hope because they don't get as much attention as arguments. Negativity gets noticed.

When engaging in social media, it can be helpful to regularly audit your intentions. Are you sharing this post because you want to archive this moment for your own personal memories? Is it to connect more deeply with friends and family? Is it to make others jealous or drum up business? To avoid misdirection, we need to ask ourselves questions and be as intentional with our online interactions with others as we are when connecting in person.

In my previous book, *Road to Wonder*, I wrote about how artists can utilize these tools for good. However, there is a downside to this ability to broadcast with the click of a button. As the barriers to posting content have come down, so has the expectation of how frequently you need to share things with the world. Algorithms reward creators not for the quality of their content, but for its frequency. This has trained a generation of creatives to share ideas as soon as they occur to them, which leads to work that is not fully developed. Quality takes time.

Pressure builds as your worth becomes tied to likes and comments. Posts are designed to create arguments because even if you don't share the author's opinion, you may still share their post, which is the most important thing. We need to release the pressure valve.

My father-in-law is a brilliant woodworker. He can create functional art out of wood, glue, and clamps. I once asked him the best lesson he had learned about creating things. He replied without hesitation, "Measure twice, cut once." There is so much wisdom in those four words. Maybe when it comes to social media, our mantra should be "Think twice, post once."

Method Four: Criticism vs. Creation

As a kid, I remember watching two guys named Siskel and Ebert when nothing else was on TV. They were like a kinder version of the two old guys I saw on *The Muppet Show* who sat in the balcony. They were the definitive film critics of their day, and in my adolescent opinion, they had the coolest jobs. Each week they would watch all the new movies and then sit and talk about what they thought about them. I would occasionally hear grown-ups discussing how they either agreed or disagreed with Siskel and Ebert's opinions. Adults would watch the show, then go see the films for themselves and form their own opinions.

Back then, we had a few critics and a lot of creators; now the opposite seems to be true. Everyone criticizes everything all the time. You can't check in on any social media platform without people blaring their opinions about everything from the clerk at the grocery store to why McDonald's should never have gotten rid of the McRib. Television has lost its viewers to YouTube, where influencers have created entire brands for themselves around reaction videos. Some of my favorite shows to watch now are YouTubers sharing their thoughts on everything from weird Christmas movies to products pushed on social media. These shows are incredibly entertaining, and the amount of work put into a single episode is fantastic.

There is, however, a strange thing that happens when creator and critic meld in this way. Unlike my parents, who would watch Siskel and Ebert critique films and then go see those movies themselves, I have found that I will watch these critiques on YouTube and adopt influencers' opinions without forming my own. In this case, the misdirection comes from me. I feel I am informed, but am I just borrowing someone else's opinion?

A big part of what makes comedy work is the comedian's perspective. Think of your favorite comedians. There is the one who claims he isn't too bright, so his comedy comes from being put in situations he doesn't always understand. Maybe you like a comedian that is always frustrated with other people and recounts stories of things that happened when he was forced to interact with others. Keep this in mind the next time you are enjoying your favorite talk show host's monologue, *Saturday Night Live* weekend update, or YouTube reaction video. If it is funny, the person is bringing a particular perspective to the conversation and adding that to the information he is presenting.

While one of the quickest ways to ruin comedy is to dissect it like a science project, examining what makes you laugh will teach you a lot about yourself. I absolutely love how comedians can share an opinion about a current issue in a way that makes us laugh and brings awareness. Let these conversations be a catalyst for your own research and discovery, and you will be less likely to be misdirected.

It is tempting to want someone else to do the work for you—to find a podcast host or YouTuber who will just create a belief system you can adopt. It can be overwhelming to sort through all the things people have to say about today's issues. For the first time in history, you can now hear what complete strangers think about current events as they are happening. At first, this way of interacting online seemed harmless. Young people shared their excitement for an upcoming music festival, parents shared that they got a great deal on a set of snow tires, and your sister posted pictures from brunch with the family. Then the arguments started. People all around the world began to use this global water cooler called the internet not just to share their opinions but to attack anyone who didn't share their perspective. Tribes began to form; people in your tribe are perceived to be right, and anyone else is seen as wrong. (Remember what I told you earlier about confirmation bias?)

These fights are different from the arguments seen in the boardroom or on the playground. Emboldened by anonymity, people are willing to say things online they would never say to another human in person. If we want social media to fulfill the promise of its name, we need to go back to square one, ask some big questions, and set some boundaries for ourselves. Does how we engage on social media reflect our values and care for others? One boundary I have applied in my own interactions is only sharing things I would be happy to have my future grandchildren read.

Method Five: Making Time Disappear

Have you ever thought, *I will just check my social media and then get to work*, and before you know it, an insane amount of time has passed? Maybe the realization hits you when your phone tells you that your screen time went up another 20 percent last week, or perhaps it was when you went for a quick bathroom break and now your legs have fallen asleep because you sat on the toilet staring at your phone for too long. It can be shocking to realize that you have scrolled your free time away, but at some point, we all realize we need something to keep us from endlessly refreshing the screen.

I have learned a lot about time theft from stealing people's watches—literally! My favorite memory of pickpocketing timepieces is when I was asked to perform at a Christmas party for the Los Angeles County Sheriff's Department.

At the time, I liked to open my show by performing close-up magic throughout the crowd, stealing several watches from people as I went so I could get everyone's attention when the show began by immediately giving their watches back. As I stepped on stage with a pocket full of watches I had stolen from half a dozen off-duty officers, I thought, *I hope they think this is funny!*

The key to stealing time is the same as stealing timepieces: First, you must entertain the audience. (How many times have you gone to check your messages online and been drawn in by funny cat videos?)

Second, you must make the participant a little self-conscious. If I can get you to think about what you are doing, you won't be thinking about what *I* am doing. We can get misdirected on social sites by thinking about why our life isn't as good as someone else's, a product that might improve that part of our appearance we don't like, or any number of other things targeted to play on our insecurities.

Third, you must change the subject and give the audience something else to focus on. This is the whole game with the scrolling—a constant feed of new information in bite-sized pieces we cannot get enough of.

Once all of this happens, stealing your time is easy because I have complete control of your attention.

The fear that we might be missing out by not constantly checking in keeps us going back, but the irony is that we are missing out on other things when we spend all our time online. When the internet first came online, data plans were limited. I remember getting a CD-ROM from Blockbuster with one hundred free AOL minutes. When you knew your time was limited, you valued it more and made the most of it. You wouldn't waste it because you knew it would cost you. Now we have all-inclusive data plans, but the reality is they may be costing us more than ever.

If you want to keep from wasting time online, you must control the distractions. It may be helpful to limit yourself to a certain amount of social media time each day. Otherwise, you will get so busy documenting life that you will forget to live it.

As we learn that misdirection can keep us from genuine connections, remember to take heart in the fact that real relationships can be cultivated. Social media is simply a tool that can be used for connection. Here are some questions that will support you in making a plan for utilizing these tools to be more authentic.

QUESTIONS TO CONSIDER REGARDING SOCIAL MEDIA

1. How do I want to use social media? Have I made a plan for this area of my life?
2. Am I truly engaging with my friends online or simply observing?
3. Do my current social media habits leave me feeling good about my life? The world in general?
4. In what ways have I personally been misdirected on social media? What, if anything, have I done to misdirect others?
5. How might doing a social media fast benefit me? What would the downside be?
6. How can I remember to think twice and post once?
7. What time limits or structures should I implement in my use of social media?

SALTSHAKER THROUGH TABLE TRICK

In any area of life, it is easy to get distracted and lose sight of what really matters. This trick is a perfect example of this type of misdirection.

The Trick

The magician tells the audience he will cause a quarter to flip from heads up to tails up without touching it. He places the coin on the table heads side up, then places a saltshaker on top of it and covers the saltshaker with an unfolded paper napkin. With a magical gesture, he declares that the coin has now flipped over and is tails side up. The spectators cannot see this because the coin is still covered by the saltshaker and the napkin. The magician asks the spectators if they would like to see it again. They agree, but before they can look, the magician makes another gesture and declares the coin has flipped again and is now heads up. The performer lifts the napkin-covered saltshaker to reveal the heads up coin, and everyone laughs at this elaborate setup for a dad joke.

Acknowledging the audience's justified disappointment, the magician quickly places the napkin-covered saltshaker over the quarter again while promising to make it up to everyone. He gives one final wave and smashes his hand down on top of the napkin, which is crushed flat onto the table. The saltshaker appears to have traveled through the solid tabletop. The magician reaches a hand under the table and retrieves the saltshaker before taking his applause.

The Secret

The key to the effect lies in the fact that a napkin will retain the shape of a saltshaker even after the saltshaker has been removed.

The coin is merely the means of misdirection. Because the audience is focused on the coin, they will be extremely surprised when the saltshaker vanishes. The secret move takes place when you remove the napkin-covered saltshaker from the quarter to show that the coin has apparently flipped back over. There is a moment when the spectators will look at the coin, allowing you to sneak the saltshaker out from under the napkin.

To do this, grab the napkin-covered saltshaker with your right hand and slide it toward the edge of the table as you point at the coin with your left hand. The spectators will look at the coin and then look you in the eye as if to say, "I get it!" When your right hand reaches the edge of the table, you will keep the napkin visible but relax your grip, allowing the saltshaker to fall past the edge of the table and onto your lap. As soon as this happens, bring the napkin—which will still retain the shape of the saltshaker—back near the coin. You can set the napkin back on top of the quarter, and it will look as though the saltshaker is still there.

All that is left to do is wave your hand over the napkin and smash it flat. Reach under the table, grab the saltshaker, and continue reaching your hand under the table until it is below the coin. Tap the saltshaker on the underside of the table, bring it out, and take your well-deserved round of applause.

To see a video breaking down how this trick is performed, visit **taylorhughes.com/misdirection**.

CHAPTER 4

MISDIRECTION IN THE WORKPLACE

When magicians want you *not* to think about something, they will distract you by making you believe something else is more important than it is. The saltshaker trick is one of the greatest dinner table tricks of all time and a perfect example of this principle at work. As the performer, you condition your audience to focus on the quarter, but it's only a distraction to make them forget about the saltshaker. The same principle can also be used in the workplace.

Method One: Saying One Thing, Doing Another

In high school, I started a band with my friends. We talked about what other bands we liked, came up with a name, designed a logo, and printed T-shirts and stickers...all before we wrote a single song.

We got so excited about the idea of being a band that we lost focus of the main thing that would make us a band: creating music.

The same thing can easily happen in our businesses. Many leadership gurus recommend starting with your *why* when launching a new business adventure. I love the idea of knowing why you are doing what you are doing, but I have found if we are not intentional, the shift from being to doing happens quickly and is rarely revisited.

Mission and vision statements traditionally are written when an organization is founded to encapsulate its core values. Core values are not hypotheticals; they are an accurate description of what the organization is designed to do and how it intends to go about it, based on the people within the organization and their values. While having words to describe the culture or environment you want to maintain is imperative, at times these cherished core values can become the quarter in the saltshaker trick. We continue to emphasize their importance with our words, but our actions, calendars, and budgets show that our priorities are in a completely different place. Those in charge are "flashing," as we magicians say—meaning that something you meant to keep hidden is visible to the audience.

The saltshaker trick reveals one of the most important keys to misdirection: pulling focus. By making you think the most important thing is the quarter, the magician can get you to put all your focus there and cause you to believe that is where their attention is also. You will assume that he is focused on the same mission you are, when his true intention is to distract you from his plan with the saltshaker. As a magician, if I want to sneak away the saltshaker without your knowing, I will downplay its importance. I want you to think it is the furthest thing from my mind. That's why people are often shocked when a leader embezzles money or runs off with their assistant. How could that person have fallen from grace when he was so focused on the mission?

Misdirection usually enters the picture when we lose sight of what we set out to do in the first place.

Method Two: Labeling People

If you are like me, it can be frustrating when something isn't in its proper place. My wife and I do our best to make sure our home is organized so everything has a spot. Knowing what to expect makes life easier. Unfortunately, though, we can take the same approach with people.

We want everyone to fit into a box because it makes dealing with them easier. So we create a box for friends and family, a box for scary people, a box for enemies, and a box for the people we think are crazy. When someone new enters our lives, we immediately begin trying to figure out where they belong. *OK, he seems nice. He does like the same sports team I do, but that ponytail looks untrustworthy.* As much as we may want to believe that everyone enters with a clean slate of possibilities, the truth is that we are making assumptions about others from the moment we meet them so we can decide how to fit them into our lives.

This is also true in the workplace. In fact, some businesses have entire processes for doing this as part of onboarding their employees. There are some fantastic tools for helping understand personality types, such as the DISC assessment or the Myers-Briggs Type Inventory. A tool popular with many churches is the Enneagram.

Business leaders will often implement this kind of testing throughout the organization. Without digging too deeply—say, getting to know their subordinates—they can mentally put them in a box.

But as with any good tool in the wrong hands, these can easily be used for harm and misdirection if the people wielding them so desire. It is easy to jump from learning about people to labeling them.

When I first entered the workforce, I had a manager who swore by a certain personality assessment. I went through the process of understanding my profile, and at first it was very helpful. I could see areas where I had strengths as well as areas where I could use improvement. The challenge came when my manager began to write off certain team members because their personality tests showed that they might struggle in a particular area.

Assessments like this can be helpful for ascertaining where the team may need more support. However, if we only give people tasks at which their profile says they will excel, we aren't giving them opportunities to grow where they may need improvement. If we assume that people are not capable of doing something because a test said it might not be their strong suit, we may be missing out on valuable insights they can bring. Good leaders don't just think about organizational productivity; they also care about empowering individuals.

Method Three: The Illusion of Input

When a magician wants to make an audience member feel that they're involved in making a particular decision—even while forcing them to choose the option the magician wants—it's called "magician's choice." In practice it looks like this:

The performer places three objects on the table: a spoon, a coffee cup, and an apple. He asks a volunteer to point at two of these items. The volunteer points at the apple and the spoon. The performer confirms, "You don't want the coffee cup? OK, we will use the apple and the spoon and get rid of the coffee cup."

We are now left with the apple and the spoon. The performer asks the volunteer to choose just one of the remaining items; he hands the performer the spoon. The performer exclaims, "Fantastic! You have eliminated everything except the apple, so that is what we will use."

In this carefully orchestrated scenario, the performer has created the illusion that the volunteer has made all the choices. The volunteer is satisfied because he was involved throughout the process and had no idea that the magician wanted him to pick the apple from the start. Moreover, no matter what decisions were made along the way, he always would have ended up with the apple.

With the magician's choice principle, the volunteer thinks everything is fair and clear but doesn't realize that the rules of the game will change based on his decisions. The magician says, "We are going to eliminate some items," but does not say if the items chosen will be eliminated or remain in play. Let's look at what would have happened if the volunteer made different decisions:

The performer places three objects on the table: a spoon, a coffee cup, and an apple. He asks a volunteer to help him decide on one of these objects, saying, "Let's eliminate some of these items. Will you pick two of them for me?" The volunteer grabs the coffee cup and the spoon. The performer asks, "Are you sure? Fantastic, you have eliminated everything except the apple, so that is what we will use."

Now let's take this scenario out of the theater and into the conference room. A vice president believes that the only way for the company to cut costs is to eliminate the community outreach program, so she holds a meeting to get "buy-in" from the team. Three programs are presented for possible elimination. The first one is an employee benefit program that will directly impact the finances of the people being asked to make the decisions. Another is to get rid of the consultants who provide team support and insights that impact the company's bottom line. The team decides to cut the outreach program after realizing they have no other choice.

The vice president never intended to cut those other programs and knew that if given the choice between these three options, the team would choose the one that impacted the company and its employees the least. The vice president gets the outcome she wanted, and the team feels as though they were involved in making the right decision. Furthermore, any fallout from this decision is then redirected to the employees because they made the call.

Managers who misdirect are often more concerned with the results they achieve than the environment they create. Meetings become a means to an end rather than an opportunity to develop and prepare future leaders.

Method Four: Keeping You Too Busy to Ask Questions
Companies are often quick to spend money by bringing in consultants to get an outside perspective—but what if we valued

giving our employees the opportunity to step outside their day-to-day activities, refresh themselves, and come back with a new perspective of their own? It is important to take time away from your work environment to refresh and see things from a different angle.

I once worked in a place that was very particular about when people could use their time off. Vacation requests always led to conversations about whether it was a good time for the organization to be without them—and in that environment, it was never a good time. Managers would use vacation requests as an opportunity to have an impromptu review meeting to discuss employees' effectiveness. Often, they would share concerns about their performance to guilt them into not taking vacation time. If they did approve time off afterward, employees would spend the time they should have been resting worrying that they might not have a job when they returned.

Manipulative leaders often fear people stepping outside the environments they control because that's where their power is limited. If we want to safeguard ourselves from manipulation, we need to be able to look at situations from different angles.

Educating yourself on different ways of seeing and being is critical to personal growth. However, unhealthy businesses want to convince you that you don't need to look elsewhere, because the way they do it is the right way. This creates a fear of outside voices that challenge the status quo. If you find yourself lacking clarity on a certain choice or are unsure whether you are in the right work environment, sometimes the best thing you can do is step away from that situation. Spend some time with other people who are not so invested in the situation, and you might just get the clarity you desire. The irony is, often your friends and family will notice it before you do because they are already seeing the situation from an outside perspective.

Breaks can be healthy. Stepping away from something in which you are deeply invested for a period will make you more effective when you return. For example, I completely walked away from magic for nearly a year. I didn't perform, practice, or think about it the entire time. When I picked it back up, I realized how many things I had attached to it that were unhelpful—like concern over what my peers thought of my performance. Before the break, I was trying hard to impress other performers and struggled with thinking I didn't really belong among them. The break gave me a new perspective on what was important and why I wanted to do magic.

Another time, I worked in an environment that encouraged employees to be ignorant of what leaders were doing. We would write off things that didn't add up by saying things like, "We don't know why every decision is being made, but we trust that the leaders know and are making choices that are best for everyone involved." If you find yourself in an environment where language like this is used, remember that you can know (or find out) what is happening in most cases by asking some bigger questions, like "Do the actions we take as an organization line up with our stated mission?" We sometimes stop asking questions because we are afraid we will appear incompetent. We may feel like it isn't our place to ask. Sometimes it's peer pressure. What if we are wrong? Remember, though, that the truth is never afraid of questions. Questioning the truth will only make it stronger, while questioning an illusion will always reveal its hidden secrets.

I am no longer surprised by how many people take extended vacations and then resign as soon as they return to work. When you are in an environment that becomes unhealthy over time, it can be difficult to recognize the changes as they are occurring. Once you spend some time out of that pressurized workspace, though, stepping back into it can be a shock to the system. When I left one very toxic workplace, it seemed like I could see the situation for what it truly was immediately afterward. I asked a friend why it took leaving for me to see clearly, and he told me it is hard to see the picture when you are standing in the frame.

If you want to avoid misdirection in business, you must keep your eyes open for scenarios like the ones we have been discussing. There is a phrase that magicians often remind each other of: "Don't run when you aren't being chased." This means that you should act naturally if you don't want to draw attention. It is built on the assumption that no one is looking for the secret thing because they are unaware of it, so don't act suspicious. If this is true, it also means that if something looks suspicious, it is worth investigating. Ask the questions.

I worked with one executive who was convinced he had all the best ideas. He organized a staff of writers to work on his speeches. At the beginning of each meeting, he would declare that he had a lot of ideas for the discussion, but he would like to hear ours first so as to not influence us. After we all shared and brainstormed, he would eventually say, "Let's go with that, and I'll save my ideas for later." But the truth was that he didn't have any original ideas of his own; he merely created the illusion that he was an idea man. This made everyone else work overtime to try to impress him with new ideas, which he would later present as his own. The people who came up with them felt proud that he used their concepts, while everyone else believed he came up with them and would applaud him.

Method Five: Putting the Onus on You

I worked in one environment where the CEO liked to keep everybody uncomfortable. He realized if we were always worried about doing the right things ourselves, we wouldn't notice when he wasn't doing the right things. The environment was highly pressurized. Expectations were immense and deadlines were always unreasonable. This created a situation in which everyone was working at peak performance, producing at a high rate, and yet never feeling like their efforts were good enough. Demanding a culture of excellence without a support structure to care for people will set your team up for failure. When groups are constantly striving for perfection, overworked and underappreciated, people begin to break down.

Ironically, the leader who cultivated that negative environment would end every meeting by saying, "Make sure you take care of yourself." I remember feeling so defeated every time I heard that. It made me feel that as an employee, if I wasn't thriving personally, it must be my fault. Managers who delegate the care of their teams to the individuals themselves are manipulating the very people they are positioned to care for. It wasn't enough that the organization said it valued self-care, because the managers continued to put structures in place to keep people from getting healthy.

Please don't take anything I've said in this chapter to mean that you can't believe people are generally good. It just means we need to be willing to ask tough questions if something seems off or if we find ourselves being pressured to make decisions that are not consistent with our values. Seeing is not always believing. The truth is that to see the good in the world, we need to believe good is possible and fight against negative ways of being and leading.

QUESTIONS TO CONSIDER FOR THE WORKPLACE

1. Is our current focus in line with our stated mission? Do our actions line up with our values?
2. Have I labeled others in a way that is unsupportive? Do I need to remove any labels that others have placed on me?
3. Do we value others' input, or are we merely creating the illusion of letting them have input?
4. Who do I need to reach out to for an outside perspective?
5. When was the last time I took a real vacation?

THE FLOATING PENCIL

In order to fight misdirection, we often need to look past what is presented to us—to find the thing behind the thing. Here is a simple illusion that takes advantage of what you cannot see.

The Trick

Next time you are sitting at the office or in a class, tell your friends that you can make a pencil float in the air using static electricity. They watch as you rub the pencil on your hand. You then hold the pencil tightly in your hand and focus intently on it, as if you are channeling some unseen power. Finally, you open your fingers to reveal the pencil suspended behind your hand.

The Secret

In order to present this illusion, you will need two pencils and a wristwatch.

Hold the first pencil in your left hand and turn so the back of your hand is facing the spectators. Hold the pencil perpendicular to the ground so that each end protrudes from the top and bottom of your closed fist. With your right hand, grab your left wrist, the fingers and thumb curled around so the audience can see them. As you concentrate on the pencil, use your right index finger to push the pencil against the palm of your left hand. At this point, you open the fingers on your left hand and the pencil will remain in place, held by your right index finger.

If you would like to add a step to this, you can place a second pencil under your watchband on your left wrist. It will go along your palm as your right finger would to hold the pencil in place. Begin the routine as before, except this time place the second pencil between your watchband and wrist before you approach the spectator. Proceed as described above, but place the pencil you intend to float between your palm and the other pencil. You can then grab your wrist as previously described. Use your index finger to cover the extra pencil and rotate your hand to show the audience you are just using your finger. Then turn back and let your right hand go completely. The pencil will remain held by the hidden pencil, and the audience will applaud.

To see a video breaking down how this trick is performed, visit **taylorhughes.com/misdirection.**

CHAPTER 5

MISDIRECTION IN POLITICS

When I was a child, my dad loved Chevrolet cars. We would cruise the neighborhood in his 1954 Chevy, and he would educate me about them whenever another Chevrolet would pass. I could tell you the year of the car based on the slight variations of the taillight design. We would attend car shows, and my dad would explain what made each one special.

His love for Chevrolets was eclipsed only by his hatred for Fords. I could tell you several dozen things my dad loves about Chevy cars, but all I know about Fords is he doesn't like them—and because of that, I have never liked Fords, either.

Unfortunately, I did the same thing with politics for years. Whatever I heard grown-ups say about a particular political party or issue, I just took that as gospel truth. I would love to tell you that when I became an adult, I reexamined those beliefs and began deciding for myself which views to hold dear. However, it wasn't until I was in my thirties that I began to see the inconsistencies between what I said I believed and how those beliefs affected the policies and politicians I supported.

Taking some time to audit your beliefs about a subject or group you choose to associate yourself with will always be beneficial. The reality is you are not the same person at forty-three that you were when you registered to vote at eighteen. Furthermore, political parties change over time. Rather than taking a brand-loyalty stance of always voting for a particular party, you may want to focus on voting based on your convictions. Remaining flexible and asking yourself tough questions is a way of safeguarding yourself against manipulation. So is listening to both sides of any argument. If we only hear one narrative about important issues, we can easily be misdirected because it means we are missing out on vital information that may change our perspective.

I admittedly know very little about sports. While most teenagers were thinking about the big game coming up, I was in my room practicing how to escape from a straitjacket. I do enjoy watching sports on TV and attending live events, but I have never understood fans who will fight each other over turf like the gangs in *West Side Story*. I often hear fans say things like, "We have to support our city!" or "These are our boys." However, most of the players didn't grow up in that city, and if at any point they receive a more lucrative offer to play somewhere else, they will jump at it. Politicians, likewise, will wear whatever jersey their constituents want in order to get people on their side, and many will unite people around a common enemy. Look out for leaders who build an audience around blaming others for the world's problems.

Hindsight is 20/20. We can all look back at times when people ended up following leaders who were clearly corrupt, and it can be easy for us to wonder how they could be so naïve. After all, Hitler convinced a lot of people it was better to be blonde when he himself was a brunette.

Leaders on both sides of the American political spectrum have lived private lives that were inconsistent with their public personas. For instance, President John F. Kennedy presented himself as a family man but was a known womanizer, and Ronald Regan took advice from his wife's astrologer while selling himself as the evangelical Christian choice. If we really care about the issues we cling to, we need to admit and address it when leaders are inconsistent with them.

Method One: Taking Advantage of Our Inattention

I heard a story about a magician who was performing for a group of his peers. He took out a handkerchief, draped it over his hand, and proceeded to shove a solid wand through it. The audience was mesmerized. This is an old idea requiring the silk to be folded in a unique way that allows for the wand to look like it is going through while it passes around the side. But this man's version was so clean that even the other magicians were amazed: He placed silk flatly over his hand and passed the wand right through as if there were a hole in the scarf.

So what was the secret?

There was a hole in the scarf.

Kids are always harder to fool than adults because they always assume the simplest answer. Adults are conditioned to think that there is no way anything could be that simple. We assume that if the trick were that easy, the magician wouldn't do it—or at the very least, he wouldn't get paid good money to perform it for us.

The same thing happens in politics constantly. We assume the candidates seeking our vote would have studied and known what they were going to discuss before they showed up at the debate or the town hall meeting. We assume they're prepared. There is no way they would just be going up there with nothing to say. It's their job to know more than we do about what's going on so they can lead us well!

We immediately give other adults a certain level of authority when they get up to speak. When it seems like they are not doing well, we will make excuses for them and say things like, "Maybe they were just having a rough night." Also, our attention spans are short, so if someone is faking it till they make it, they only have to fake it as long as we are paying attention. (We may pull out our phones, after all.) The easier it is to distract someone, the easier that person is to manipulate.

We see this during televised debates. A candidate gives an insufficient answer to a question, so the moderator rephrases it and once again receives a less-than-adequate response. Because of time limits, the moderator moves on and the question is never answered. We move on as an audience and forget about this inconsistency. Sometimes we just have to push back a little harder to keep from being misdirected.

A well-known magician named Billy McComb used to perform a classic trick in which he would take out a spool of thread and tear off a length about five feet long. He would then tear that into smaller pieces before restoring all of them into one as he stretched his arms out wide. Once, he was performing in a large hall for a group of magicians, long before video projection would allow a close-up view of what he was doing, and the audience was seated far from the stage. This routine was one of his signature pieces, and people would expect to see it—but this time, his spool of thread was empty. So he simply went on stage and mimed the whole routine without the thread. Everyone in the audience just assumed they were the only people who couldn't see the thread, and gave him a standing ovation.

When we assume that people in authority are doing what they promised and stop asking questions, misdirection abounds. If the people we voted for don't seem to know what they're talking about or aren't delivering results, then we think we must be at fault. We assume the thread is there, but sometimes they're just working from an empty spool.

Remember the story about the emperor's new clothes? The focus is usually on the ruler and his foolishness—the vanity it took to believe that only the smart and worthy people could see the invisible clothes the swindlers had made for him, and thus, he paraded naked through the streets. But what about all the people around the emperor who couldn't see the clothes either, but said nothing and allowed the parade to happen? They were accomplices. Sure, misdirection sometimes takes us completely by surprise, but there are other times when we know all along things are going to hit the fan. Yet we go along with it. Perhaps we are afraid of what will happen to us if we speak up. You may be afraid of losing your job, your community, even your identity. It always costs us something when we choose not to be an accomplice in misdirecting others.

Magicians take advantage of the spectators' perspective to accomplish many of their tricks. I have attended training workshops dedicated to better understanding site angles and knowing when vision will be impaired by perspective. Try this now: Look straight ahead and hold your hand flat in front of your face about ten inches from your nose. Imagine a line being drawn parallel to the floor between your hand and your nose. If you slowly lift your hand straight up without moving your head, you will notice the moment when it passes out of your line of sight. If you drew a line from the center of your eyeball to your eyebrows and continued at that angle, you could see anything below the line without moving your head, but anything above it would be out of your sight.

With that in mind, if a magician wanted to do something sneaky without you seeing, he wouldn't need to do it behind his back; he just needs to do it out of your line of sight. We all have a limited field of view; if you are aware of other people's blind spots, you can use them to your advantage. This means that political parties that understand your perspective can market toward it. This is the problem with not seeing life from different perspectives.

A huge part of performing, whether you are a comedian or a magician, is audience management. Have you ever been to a show and seen a performer call out someone who was on their phone? This may be because it was distracting to the comedian, but it is also a fantastic way to encourage people to stay off their phones during the show. If I see someone get called out for doing something, I am less likely to do that thing myself. The more we pay attention, the harder it is to be fooled.

It's always important to ask big questions about who is funding the news programs you watch, but even more so during political campaigns. Who is buying the commercial slots? Why was this the time they wanted to buy? Sometimes it's easy to tell, and sometimes it's not. If there's an ad you're not sure about, watch it all the way to the end and look for the fine print that begins, "Paid for by So-and-So." Then go to the internet and look up that group. There are people who have a lot to gain from ensuring you believe what they want you to.

Method Two: Avoiding the Real Issues

I once attended a conference where a speaker was introduced as an expert in his field. It was obvious that the hosts were honored to have such a knowledgeable presenter there. The gentleman walked to the center of the stage, dressed to impress, carrying himself with confidence. He spoke with authority and passion as he addressed the crowd . . . but it turned out he knew absolutely nothing about the subject he'd been asked to speak about.

He began to weave a tapestry of mismatched words, ideas, and illustrations that sounded like he knew what he was talking about, but they didn't add up. He turned out to be an entertainer, a professional "double talker" who was hired to make a point about how important it is to communicate clearly. The audience loved him; I was shocked by how good he was at bluffing. After that, I began to pay closer attention to people presented as "experts."

Our shortened attention spans have set us up to be more easily misdirected. We are so bombarded with information that it is much easier now for politicians to fake their way along. We need leaders with authenticity, experience, and accountability. It can seem daunting as a constituent to think about how we can change things for the better, but one important way is to seek out and support leaders who have good character. We don't need people who can play the part; we need people of strong conviction. All too often we see politicians who use these kinds of verbal gymnastics to avoid the issues that are important to the people they are elected to serve.

There is a sea creature called the mimic octopus. While its body looks like that of a typical octopus, it can disguise, contort, and fold its body to take the shape of at least fifteen other animals to protect itself from predators. Politicians who sway back and forth to please everyone are like this. They focus on getting elected; then when they are in office, they focus on getting reelected. Rather than doing what is best for the people they represent, they do whatever it takes to protect themselves.

Method Three: Ignoring the Facts

In high school, I had a friend who worked at Baskin-Robbins. After school, I would often swing by the shop to see what new flavors I could sample using the all-powerful friends-and-family discount. One Thursday in March, I walked into the shop expecting to see the new flavors and instead stumbled upon a crime scene: There was my buddy, covered from head to toe in what appeared to be melted ice cream. In fact, the entire wall behind him, the floor, and the ceiling looked like a weird modern art splatter painting. Stunned, I asked him what had happened.

Apparently, one of his regulars had come in wearing her workout clothes, which was not unusual since the shop shared a parking lot with a gym. What was strange to my friend was that this woman had been coming in every day for the last month after her workout to order an extra-large Cappuccino Blast. Both the gym and the ice cream shop had walls with floor-to-ceiling windows, so my friend could see the woman running intently on the treadmill that faced the shop every day, as if she were staring at her motivation. *Just one more mile, Denise, and you get another taste of that frozen mocha goodness!*

That day, after my pal had made the woman's standard order and handed it to her, she commented that she couldn't believe she was gaining weight. She had been working out intently and drinking "these protein shakes" every day. My friend felt compelled to share the truth that Cappuccino Blasts from Baskin-Robbins are not protein shakes; they're mostly ice cream, and that was most likely the reason Denise wasn't meeting her goal. At first, she laughed, thinking he was joking, but then she realized he was telling the truth. Finally, in anger, she lobbed the thirty-two-ounce ice cream grenade at him and stormed off as it exploded all over the shop.

I am not sure where this lady got the idea that ice cream shakes were good for her. Perhaps she misheard a commercial. Maybe a friend passed on that false information. She may have even stolen someone's treadmill at the gym, and convincing her to buy these shakes was his retaliation. All I know is that she believed false information that hurt her in the long run.

Another way to ensure we aren't being misdirected is to go to the source of the info. Is this thing that I believe actually true? We must take personal responsibility for what we believe instead of blaming others.

Method Four: Blaming the Victim

I had a friend growing up whose dad would completely lose it when he got angry, with a zero to sixty level of intensity that would always end the same way. After completely shocking his family with a frustrated outburst, he would say, "Why do you make me treat you like this?" Manipulators often blame their victims for their own negative actions.

Recently, I performed at a comedy club. For whatever reason, the comic who was on before me was struggling to connect with the audience. He finally resorted to telling them that they were the problem.

There is an old saying in the entertainment business that there is no such thing as a bad audience, meaning a performer is responsible to give his best regardless of how the audience reacts. While I agree with this, I also can tell you that not every audience is prepared to be an audience. Often, people may have just walked past the venue and seen that a show was taking place. These patrons' expectations and anticipation levels are very different than what they might have been had they known about the show and bought tickets in advance. Other times, one person really wants to see the show, but drags along a group of buddies who aren't that interested. And sometimes the audience just doesn't connect with you as a performer.

I have learned the hard way that it is better not to overthink this, but just do the best I can and then get off the stage. Some entertainers go the other route by insulting the audience or saying, "The last crowd loved this, what's wrong with you all?" It took me years to learn that this is rarely effective; even if it leads to laughs, it does not lead to the audience wanting to see you again. We are often tempted to blame someone else when things don't go our way. What always brings me back from that brink is remembering that I am responsible for my performance.

Like comedians who turn on their audience, politicians often play the victim by blaming the actual victims. We should be cautious when we hear someone in authority constantly pointing the finger at others, especially when the authority figure blames someone in a weaker position. Many political candidates attack their opponents rather than sharing why they would be best for the job. The priority for all political parties is choosing someone who is electable, not necessarily someone who would be effective. Politicians rally around stopping a common enemy rather than moving the nation forward.

If voting the party line requires you to support leaders who are inconsistent with your values, it may be time to ask yourself if that is a party you want to attend.

Method Five: Of the People, by the People, for the People

Other than the time I was in college and an epic prank battle nearly led to the entire neighborhood being covered in bathroom tissue, I typically spend very little time thinking about toilet paper. However, during the pandemic when suddenly we could not find it anywhere, we all spent an incredible amount of time, energy, and money acquiring this precious resource.

What you think matters most changes based on your needs. Older, wealthy individuals may think that lower taxes are the most important thing to fight for politically. Meanwhile, younger students may think that affordable education is critical. Yet any honest politician will tell you the question shouldn't be merely "What is best for me?" but "What is best for society?" We need to examine how much of our belief systems are based on what benefits us directly.

This book is not just about recognizing misdirection when it comes from others; it is also about taking personal responsibility for our own ways of being and believing. A good question to ask is whether your beliefs cost you anything, or whether they only benefit you personally. When we talk about our beliefs, we tend to correlate them with facts. We choose to vote for things we believe are true. However, if all your beliefs benefit you, isn't that a little suspicious? At the very least, it is an incredible coincidence that you happen to be in the exact situation that would improve from people voting in the way you believe is right. For example, Calvinism is a branch of Christianity that believes Jesus died for a limited number of "elect" people—but I have never met any Calvinists who don't believe themselves to be part of that elect group.

Truth should not be relative to your circumstances. If we are genuinely considering the welfare of others and not just our own, our beliefs will sometimes inconvenience our lives. In those moments, the question becomes whether our beliefs will affect our actions, or whether we will bend our beliefs to justify our actions. We talk a lot in the United States about the sacrifices others made to ensure our freedom. If we don't want to slip while passing the baton, we need similar selfless conviction and commitment to doing the right thing even when it doesn't directly benefit us.

Think back to when your high school held the annual election for student body president. There was always one candidate who was an outlier, who had researched solutions to major issues the school was facing. No one ever took that person seriously. Instead, they were mesmerized by the good-looking kid who entered the cafetorium to the song "We Will Rock You" while throwing out free candy and claiming they would put a soda machine in the quad. High school politics were not much different from the politics we see today. Politicians only have the power that voters give them. So why is it that sometimes we see people who follow manipulative leaders with cult-like devotion?

To tackle this question, let's dive into a subject everyone has heard of but very few know about: hypnosis. You may have heard a friend share that he was able to stop smoking because of hypnosis, or perhaps you attended a company party where the boss was hypnotized and squawked like a chicken. Maybe you saw a person with a fantastic mustache wave a pocket watch in front of someone to make them pass out on TV—but were these people really acting outside of their own control?

There are two basic forms of hypnosis: clinical hypnosis, known as hypnotherapy, and stage hypnosis, which is generally only performed for entertainment purposes. Hypnosis occurs when someone follows specific prompts to enter a very relaxed state. This trance-like state does not take away their self-control; on the contrary, it is a state of deep focus and concentration. People are more attuned to what is going on and therefore are more likely to be open to suggestions.

When someone is hypnotized, he still makes all his own decisions about what to do. This is very important to remember: In either a clinical or onstage environment, the person being hypnotized must *want* to be hypnotized. You cannot be hypnotized against your will. Also, the fact that you want to be hypnotized doesn't necessarily mean you will experience it.

Stage hypnotists spend a good part of their shows qualifying participants. They begin by asking the audience a series of questions, then bring a large group on stage and slowly dismiss the people who don't seem like they will participate freely. Three groups are left. The first doesn't become hypnotized, and those people are dismissed. The second is a group of people who do experience hypnosis.

The third group consists of volunteers who want to be hypnotized, but don't actually experience hypnosis. However, because they have never been hypnotized, they aren't aware that it isn't happening, so they just play the part. Often these are the people who do the most outrageous things and make the show memorable.

Political debates can be mesmerizing. When a topic is presented, we quickly take a side, and the conversation becomes about winning and proving what we already thought rather than exploring other possibilities. These conversations that are meant to be about finding solutions to shared problems end up separating us further and solidifying existing (often misdirected) beliefs. At a certain point, our reaction time is quicker, our reasoning goes out the window, and it all becomes about defending our side. Unhealthy leaders will look for opportunities to build on this tension and would have us start seeing our neighbors as our enemies. It is possible to engage in healthy debate without going to war with one another, but that requires all of us making sure we don't get carried away by the showbiz of it all.

What if the next time we enter the voting booth, we hit the pause button long enough to reexamine our intentions and ask ourselves if the way we have been engaging in politics is truly in line with what we believe and who we want to be. Are we holding the politicians we support to our own standards, or have we chosen sides and are just voting the party line? One of the best ways to stay true to what we believe is to challenge those beliefs on occasion.

QUESTIONS TO CONSIDER ABOUT POLITICS

1. Do the candidates I support have integrity?
2. Am I voting for what is best for society or only for what benefits me personally?
3. What drives my political decisions more—love for others or fear of loss?
4. What is an area where I need to be paying more attention?
5. What if I am wrong?
6. Have I allowed myself to be hypnotized by the "game" of politics without truly thinking it through?
7. Have I looked at all the sides?
8. Have things changed in the last decade while I was busy [raising my family, getting an advanced degree, etc.]? Have I moved past brand loyalty to truly consider the party platform?
9. Which groups are paying for political commercials? Which are paying for seemingly innocuous ads about American business or lifestyles?
10. Have I learned to recognize double-talk?

CUT AND RESTORED ROPE

For as long as the rope has existed, magicians have been cutting it in half and putting it back together. The cut-and-restored-rope trick is a crowd-pleaser that is easy to perform with a little practice. It is accomplished not by fixing something, but by convincing viewers that a perfectly solid object is broken. While we all have areas we would like to improve or change in our lives, some of us have been taken advantage of by people who have convinced us that we are broken. Fixing things that are not broken is a major method of misdirection.

The Trick

The magician brings out a piece of rope about five feet long and holds both ends in his left hand, allowing the middle loop to hang down. He then takes a pair of scissors from his pocket, brings the middle of the rope up with them, and cuts it in half. With a snap of the fingers, the two pieces of rope are restored to one. The magician holds the stretched-out rope between his hands as the audience applauds.

The Secret

There are several versions of this trick, but the one I am teaching you is my favorite because the method is so diabolical: You never actually cut the rope.

Instead, you begin with an extra piece of rope that is about eight inches long. Hold this small piece in your right hand so that it is folded in half with the loop toward your thumb and the two small ends pointing down toward your pinky finger. The audience is unaware that this piece is palmed in your right hand as you bring out a five-foot length of rope and have a volunteer inspect it. To the audience, it appears that you have one solid length of rope while the extra little piece goes unnoticed. Take the long rope back from the volunteer and hold it in your outstretched hands. Your left hand holds one end while your right hand holds the other end, as well as the hidden extra piece.

Now bring your hands together. As you do, place both ends of the long rope in your left hand so that they remain visible and the large loop hangs freely below. With your right hand, bring the middle of the long rope up and into your left hand. Leave the actual loop of the long rope hidden in your left palm as you transfer the extra hidden piece into your left hand so that the loop sticks up and the two small ends are clipped at the left fingertips.

Remove a pair of scissors from your pocket and cut the loop of the small piece in half. This will look to the audience like you have just cut the long piece in half. At this point, you will be left with the center of the long rope tucked into the bottom of your left hand and all four ends sticking out the top of your left hand. Trim the small ends again so that the pieces fall to the ground and all that remains is the solid five-foot length of rope.

To restore the rope, simply make a magical gesture and grab one end in each hand. As you stretch your hands apart, allow the center of the rope to fall; it will appear as if the rope has been restored.

To see a video breaking down how this trick is performed, visit **taylorhughes.com/misdirection.**

CHAPTER 6

MISDIRECTION IN THE CHURCH

It can seem like every time you turn on the news, there is a story about another scandal at a religious organization. It is disheartening to see good causes and individuals negatively impacted by the manipulation of those tasked with serving them. From the Catholics to the Baptists to Hillsong, it seems no faith tradition has gone unscathed. How does this keep happening? How do you know which organizations you can trust?

While these methods of misdirection can and are applied across different faith expressions, I will focus on the evangelical church in America, since that is where most of my experience has been. I've seen a systematic problem with misdirection in the evangelical church today, and it needs to be addressed.

Method One: Mission Drift

Every organization exists for a purpose. A good starting point to see if misdirection may be present is to ask if the organization's actions line up with its stated mission and core values. If it says the organization is all about people, but all the focus is on programming, misdirection may be at hand.

When you were a kid, did you ever play the telephone game? A large group would sit in a circle, and one person would whisper something to the person on their left. It could be as simple as "I have a dog whose daughter is my granddog." The person on the left would then repeat that phrase to the person next to them; by the time it got all the way around the circle, the results were usually shockingly different, like "Balance on a log in the London fog." This could be a result of people mishearing the person before them, interpreting it to mean something else, or just deciding to say something different because they wanted to get a better reaction.

This also happens in storytelling. As stories are reshared and passed along, they are improved upon or edited based on the results the storyteller received the last time he told it. Sometimes swapping a single word can change the way people respond.

If you choose to follow a specific religion, it is important to look at the foundations of that belief system and not just the words of the current leaders. There are currently more than forty-five thousand different Christian denominations in the world, all of whom claim to follow Jesus.[1] However, many of them have found different ways to interpret Scripture and its meaning for us today. This impacts the way they think about everything from social issues to clothing. We must ask where our beliefs come from. If you say you follow Jesus, do your beliefs actually line up with His words, or are they the result of a two-thousand-year-long game of telephone?

In the church where I grew up, we said the mission was to go into all the world with the Gospel, but in practice, it was all about bringing people to our weekend service. And what a service it was! I'm talking about stadium seating, intelligent lighting, and state-of-the-art sound—a full theatrical experience. We hired professional musicians who didn't have to share our faith as long as they had the look and sound our leaders wanted.

While I love theatrics—remember, I am the guy who sings show tunes in public—I believe we need to be careful that the tools used to create an ambience don't cross the line into manipulation. Lighting a room in a certain way creates anticipation. Certain chord progressions build suspense. It may be possible that the moment you feel like God is moving might just be a perfectly timed key change in the music. Environments like these can become breeding grounds for spiritual manipulation if we aren't careful.

As a magician, saying one thing and doing another is part of the game. You clearly say you are putting the coin in your left hand while keeping it in your right hand. This small deception leads to elation and joy when we are surprised to see the coin has vanished. However, when spiritual leaders take this approach, it leads to disillusionment.

Many churches built on the idea of sacrificing to serve others falter when they realize they cannot attract the amount of people or money they want with that kind of focus—so they look for other ways to bring people in. (Sacrifice is a hard sell.) Church services shift from being gatherings built on worshiping God and empowering the congregation to love their communities to entertaining people and creating an illusion of impact. We need the best music, the latest technology, and the most attractive-looking people on stage.

With coffee shops in the lobby and other amenities, it's now hard to tell the difference between many churches and social clubs. People are willing to attend and give money—not to serve others, but because of how the church is serving them. Instead of being an expression of love, the offering plate becomes a bill for services rendered.

The idea of passing on what you have experienced with God is central to the teachings of Christianity. The early Church was trained to take it into the world. However, in contemporary American Christianity, the goal often seems like it is less about going out to love others than getting them to come to church so they can experience love. It is easy to leave the building feeling like we have changed the world, but did we actually do any of the things we discussed? We are left with the illusion of impact—and misdirection has happened once again.

A major way the modern church builds community is by establishing small groups in which people can make new friends and support one another. To this day, many of my closest friends are people I met through groups like these. However, if it's used as a one-stop-shop approach for building community, it can actually pull us away from people with whom we already have natural connections. The best church small groups are safe spaces where people can connect and grow. For individuals who have left negative or dangerous situations, this can be incredibly helpful. However, it is easy for church small groups to begin with the purpose of loving friends, coworkers, neighbors, and families but after awhile, slip into creating forced relationships. Ultimately, this doesn't achieve the intended purpose.

Method Two: Worshiping the Pastor

The Wizard of Oz tells the story of four friends who go on a journey together to find something they each feel is missing from their lives: The Tin Man doesn't have a heart and believes that if he did, he would be able to love. The Scarecrow doesn't have a brain and is certain he would be better off if he could improve his thinking. The Lion needs courage, and poor Dorothy just wants to find her way back home to Kansas.

All these needs are natural human desires. There is nothing wrong with wanting to be thought of as brave, smart, and loving. There is nothing wrong with wanting a home. Where this band of seekers goes wrong is placing their hopes in a person, the Wizard, believing he can solve all their problems. We later find out that the Wizard isn't all he was made out to be—just a man spinning wheels to keep the illusion of "the Wizard" alive. Sadly, he is just another human who doesn't have all the answers.

The Wizard himself appears to be exhausted from keeping up this charade. However, it is the only thing he knows, and so he keeps perpetuating the lie. The Wizard is insecure. He has found himself in an impossible situation. He convinces himself that letting people know who he truly is will do more harm than good, so he struggles along in solitude with no way out.

This story is being played out in churches across America today. Pastors repeatedly fall into this trap of being the all-knowing and all-powerful "Wizard." Some of them seek that kind of power and control; many others don't, but are playing by the rules of the game nonetheless. Either way, if we want to stop seeing people fall from pedestals, we need to stop placing them there in the first place. We elevate individuals to unreasonably high standards of excellence and create platforms that cannot carry the weight we place upon them.

Method Three: Unhealthy Leadership CULTure

Throughout the 1980s and '90s, megachurches became more popular. Until then, many believed that once a church reached a certain size, it would be hard for the pastor to shepherd the congregation and for true community to exist. Therefore, people attended local churches near their homes, where they would fellowship with their actual neighbors. But as numerical growth became a major focus, the resources allocated to making the facility a destination increased. More people at church equals more church income and the ability to provide more amenities. So people began commuting to church, driving past a dozen others to attend one that had "more to offer." Churches began raising money for larger buildings, new children's wings, and television cameras to bring in even more people.

The church in America has become big business, and many of them are run that way. Pastors are no longer busy with hospital visits and community dinners; they are managing personnel, watching budgets, and brainstorming programs. The pastor is now, for all intents and purposes, a CEO. Instead of focusing on reading and interpreting Scripture, staff learn the latest growth techniques from entrepreneurs so they can support the spiritual enterprise. In unhealthy environments, leadership meetings can focus on developing a culture to influence and control the staff and volunteers.

In this type of culture, one of the unwritten rules is "If you aren't with us, you are against us." Once staffers question authority or ask for accountability, they begin to be viewed as a problem.

In spiritually abusive environments, "no" is never presented as an option. Staffers are expected to play the game—and meanwhile, the congregation has no idea about the back-office intrigues. The entire culture becomes steeped in fear. When people are afraid, they will do things they normally would not. And even if they didn't fear failing their leaders, those people definitely do not want to fail God. The pressure to be perfect because anything less would be displeasing to God is a big deal in many religious institutions. It is strange how much time is spent talking about pleasing God as if His love for us is based on our accomplishments.

I was taught that God loves us unconditionally, knows we aren't perfect, and forgives us for our mistakes; this theology is used to draw people to church. Who wouldn't want to believe a message that graceful? However, the theology in many modern churches tends to change after someone joins to focus on what that person is doing. *Are you giving? Are you serving?*

Be wary of any leaders or environments that are less concerned with the state of your relationship with God than with the amount you are giving or the time you are spending in service.

Method Four: Fear Rules

Faith, hope, and love are considered to be the three most important theological virtues of Christianity, the greatest of these being love. But when auditing the modern American church, while you will see a huge emphasis placed on faith, there is very little hope being preached today, and there is often an absence of love in action. One sign that a congregation may be operating without hope is when the messaging centers around fear and guilt. Unhealthy leaders will try to guilt you into attending, guilt you into serving, and guilt you into giving. Furthermore, they will instill fear of the consequences that come from not following through with these commitments: God won't bless you, or leaders won't approve of you.

Manipulative leaders hold themselves at a distance from the congregation and use their presence as a reward. Employees become desperate to win their approval. If you want to break people down, you simply must make them feel they will never be accepted.

In churches, the pastor or senior leader can take on the role of a father figure, which makes seeking his approval even more important. When a leader gives you a role, it makes you feel important. Conversely, the threat of having that job taken away if he becomes unhappy with you is stressful.

You can tell a lot about an organization by the way people there talk about former members. When longtime volunteers and staff just vanish, it is easy to assume they did something wrong. Furthermore, when most of the congregants' relationships are proximity-based, when people leave, it is "out of sight, out of mind." Unhealthy leaders encourage this type of disconnection. This trains those who remain in the congregation to believe that if they disagree with the leaders, the same thing will happen to them. People won't question things for fear of losing their community and reputation.

Method Five: Follow the Money

In the early 1900s, famed magician Harry Houdini went on a legitimate spiritual quest after his mother died, trying to find a psychic who could reach beyond the grave to help him connect with her. In his search for a real connection, however, he discovered that so-called mediums were using many of the same techniques he was using onstage. He was devastated and ended up exposing many false prophets of his day in order to prevent them from taking advantage of others. This type of spiritual manipulation is still happening today and takes on many forms.

I don't share any of this to discourage generosity or working with organizations that are doing amazing work. I have had the honor of partnering with some phenomenal organizations that are wisely stewarding their resources to positively impact families and communities. However, I have also witnessed firsthand what can happen when narcissistic leaders see the generosity of others as a tool for their own gain.

The stats on church donations vary, but almost all show that the amount given in churches in America each year far surpasses the amount that would be required to address global hunger.[2] So what exactly are you paying for?

The prosperity gospel is the idea that God's will is for people to experience material wealth; if you aren't experiencing abundance in your finances, you must not be following God's will. Therefore, if you just serve, give money to the church, and do what the pastor says, you will experience this prosperity. Some go as far as to say that there is a spiritual contract: if you do all the right things, God is *required* to bless you.

This is another trap built on our desire to be successful and happy. Our spiritual questions become less about understanding God and our purpose than about what God can do to help us fulfill our desires. I have attended more than one church conference where the speaker promoted this prosperity gospel and also interviewed leaders of an organization that fed impoverished children within one hour-long session.

If we want to safeguard ourselves and others giving to churches or charities, we must ask where the money is going.

I worked with one church that held entire meetings on how to phrase things during the collection of money. For instance, if we had a guest speaker, we would plan to take a second collection during the service to offset his honorarium. But since not all the money collected during the offering was earmarked for that, we had to phrase things a certain way to make up for both collections. For example: "Well, isn't it an honor to have Pastor Martin visiting with us today? We want to be able to bless him just as he has blessed us, so we are going to take a special *missions* offering right now. This will allow us to support our speaker today, just as we support all our other speakers."

If you don't read too much into this announcement, you might think that whatever you put in the offering plate is going to the guest—but this is not necessarily true.

If you give to an organization rather than an individual, it can be helpful to ask some questions about how those funds are allocated. Organizations like Charity Navigator provide statistics on charities, such as the percentage of your donation that goes to overhead.

Method Six: Professional Believers

When I was growing up in the evangelical church in the 1980s, there was a lot of talk about how Hollywood celebrities were the biggest threat to Christianity. If we weren't careful, these false prophets might distract us from the cause. As a result, new celebrities began to pop up within the church. Many pastors began to build followings, obtain book deals, and make millions off of their built-in audiences. They became influencers, and the worlds of celebrity and church melded together.

These Christian celebrities say their expensive clothes and cars are a result of trusting God. TV preachers claim this is all the result of their sacrifice and obedience, when it was the generosity of others that filled the offering plate and provided for their lavish lifestyle. The world of Christian celebrities is full of disgraced individuals who did not practice what they preached. So why do we continue to be attracted to people who emphasize wealth and status while claiming to follow Jesus's example of ultimate sacrifice and humility?

As children, we are taught to wonder and explore. Parents watch with joy as their children experience a new food for the first time or interact with a pet. Kids ask questions about everything. *Why is the sky blue? Are we there yet? Why can't I have a cookie?* We have all either given or received the frustrated response, "Because I said so." The reason this response is bad is that it comes from exhaustion. Even a parent who is overjoyed to see their child learning will inevitably become tired of the constant questioning. For years I took this approach in the church I belonged to; I had lots of questions but realized that in that culture, questioning was not valued as much as loyalty.

We can all grow tired of asking questions. This may be because we find we don't like the answers, or worse, we know we will become responsible for whatever we learn. It's easy to stop asking questions, choose a leader, and just do whatever that person says. However, if we want real change, we need to do things differently. Never stop asking questions, and demand accountability from people who are in a position to oversee others. If manipulation is happening, the signs will be there. You just need to know what to look for.

QUESTIONS TO CONSIDER ABOUT CHURCH

1. What type of world do I want to invest in?
2. Does this church's actions line up with its stated mission?
3. Does being involved here help me love people more?
4. How does the church handle money?
5. What accountability structures are in place?
6. Is there a lot of guilt and fear in the sermons?
7. Does this church expect to become my sole community?
8. Is fame important to my pastor?
9. Is the lead pastor involved in the community, or does the connection end at the footlights of the stage?

COIN THROUGH ARM

As you can see, a lot of misdirection happens when people do one thing and say another. This trick hinges on being able to act like something is happening that isn't. For this, you will need any coin, a flat surface, and a spectator seated across from you.

The Trick

Borrow a coin from your spectator and declare that you will cause it to pass visibly into your arm. With your sleeves rolled up, place your left elbow on the table and hold your left fist straight up as you hold the coin in the fingertips of your right hand. You begin by rubbing the coin slowly on your left arm, but nothing happens. You try again, and still nothing happens. You accidentally drop the coin, but you don't give up. On your third try, the coin appears to pass right through your skin and into your left arm. You show your right hand to be empty and declare that you will make the coin reappear from behind your ear, then reach up and grab it from behind your left ear.

At this point, the volunteer will ask to see the trick again, but remember, a magician never repeats a trick.

The Secret

The secret to this lies in the fact that you pretended to make a mistake by dropping the coin. When you drop the coin from your right hand, you appear to quickly reach down with your left hand, grab the coin, and place it back in your right hand. Your left hand then goes back up next to your face as you rub the coin against your left arm with your right hand. But in reality, you never put the coin back in your right hand. When you drop it, you grab it with your left hand and only pretend to put it back into your right hand. You keep the coin in your left hand for the rest of the routine. All you need to do to complete the illusion is mime rubbing the coin along your left forearm with your right hand and pretend it has passed into your arm. Reach up with your left hand, which still has the coin in it, and pretend to take it from behind your ear.

To see a video breaking down how this trick is performed, visit **taylorhughes.com/misdirection.**

MISDIRECTION IN THE NEIGHBORHOOD

It's interesting that two popular children's television shows of the 1970s focused on the concept of community. *Mister Rogers' Neighborhood* had some great lessons about the importance of building connections with our diverse neighbors. *Sesame Street* was set in a bustling New York City neighborhood with shops and friends and other goings-on. Both emphasized the importance of caring for the people around us and ensuring that we curate environments where everyone can thrive and experience love.

Misdirection is possibly most detrimental when it hits home with our neighbors and family members. Let's take a look at how misdirection may be affecting our closest relationships these days.

Method One: Pretending

Family should be the one group of people with whom we can be ourselves. The people who have known us the longest just get who we are, right? It seems that every holiday season you hear people talking about going home for the holidays—but why do these accounts sound less like joyous occasions than terrifying survival stories?

It seems like my friends are telling me about the turmoil they are seeing in their families much more often these days. Years ago, we all had at least one family member with whom we would laugh and say, "Ha! You're so crazy!" Now we look at them and think "Oh! They *are* so crazy."

When you are a kid, home is where you are your truest self. You watch your favorite TV shows, wear your comfiest clothes, and blast your favorite guilty-pleasure tunes unashamedly. But at some point, you leave the house, and this is when you start to learn how to not fully be yourself. You are encouraged to sit quietly and act properly. Unintentionally, you are taught that to be accepted in public, you need to pretend, or at the very least, adjust your personality.

Later you go to school, where you learn the version of your public persona that works best for the setting. You start to wear different versions of yourself like interchangeable masks. You are one way in class, one way with your friends, one way at church, and another way at home with the family. This is part of the growing-up process, but it also begs the question, *Where can we be our truest self?*

We spend a lot of time trying to find groups to fit into; we go to great lengths to find acceptance. (I still have the Hypercolor

T-shirt I wore as a kid to try to look cool. The idea of a shirt that changed colors when it got hot or cold was great—until recess, when it highlighted exactly where you had sweat the most.) One group we should fit into easily is our family—but when we don't allow people to be themselves at home, they will find replacement families elsewhere.

For many years, I worked with students in a youth group who felt that way. This caused confusion and friction at home. In my talks with these kids, I heard that their parents either didn't understand them or didn't approve of who they were as individuals. When they realized they couldn't get approval at home, they sought out a group of people who would validate them.

If all goes well, when you reach adulthood, you venture out to live life on your own—not completely isolated, but with much less influence from the family of your birth. This can be a challenging thing for parents to realize: If you succeed at parenting, your children will leave you eventually.

This is where the dynamic begins to change. You go from testing boundaries during adolescence to being completely in charge of your own choices. As children, we don't decide what type of traditions we will have, what religion we are raised with, or what our family's political perspectives will be. We are born into a functioning ecosystem, and we accept our family's perspective and dynamics as the norm.

But in adulthood, you are introduced to other ways of viewing the world. You continue to grow and make choices about your own values as you move forward. You start to decide which of your family's beliefs you will keep and which don't seem to fit anymore. Like hand-me-down clothes, you wear these beliefs for a while and are grateful for the gift, but at some point, you realize they were never yours to begin with. You develop into a different person.

Meanwhile, the rest of your family is on their own journey of discovery. Siblings go off to work or school, make new friends, travel, and develop their unique perspectives. Your parents likewise adjust to a life that is no longer focused on raising children and revisit their own perspectives.

And then you all get together for a holiday. An assortment of individuals who have been on completely different journeys and who now may have wildly different perspectives come back together and try to celebrate the way they did as children. No wonder there is conflict!

It isn't so much that your family grew apart; it is just that you were apart while you all were growing. This doesn't mean that you can't stay close and connected; the misdirection comes in when we try to act like we haven't changed in order to get along. Sometimes we disguise ourselves as the same people we were years ago because if our families see us for who we really are, they won't accept us.

This keeps us from having meaningful relationships with our families of origin as adults. Think for a moment about the things you have changed your mind about in the last ten years. These topics might include the parts of your life that you feel define who you are as an individual now—and yet, when we gather with family, we say things like, "Don't talk about religion or politics." One way we can avoid misdirection at home is to make a commitment to not wear masks in front of one another and give people a safe place to be the truest version of themselves.

Method Two: Making Up Stories to Help Us Cope with the Truth

Is there a difference between lying and withholding information? I suppose it depends on your intention in doing so. Most people would not say they are liars, but we all withhold information that might give an unflattering picture of the situation sometimes.

Perhaps you promised your wife you would start eating healthy foods, and when she asks what you ate that day, you tell her you had black coffee and a banana. While this is true, you didn't mention you also had a breakfast burrito and a pint of ice cream. (That last example may or may not be a personal confession.) These types of fibs start small but can have big consequences when the stakes are higher. But when the stakes get higher, we tend to want to stretch the truth even more.

Making sure we are honest with each other will safeguard the family from misdirection.

I experienced some familial misdirection for most of my life. My grandmother was an incredible person. She was very active in her church and would read the Bible each morning as soon as she woke up. She was a wonderful neighbor and friend, the first person many people would call when they needed help. She was also very proper: She loved going to tea and would use any excuse to decorate something in the house with a doily. She carried herself with dignity and encouraged us to use our manners.

A couple of times a year, my family would make the twelve-hour trek to spend time with her and my grandfather in southern Oregon. I adored every visit to their house. Whether playing in the creek that ran through their front yard or going out to breakfast with them and their elderly friends, each day was memorable.

However, we kids knew very little of my grandmother's story. I knew that she had moved a lot and that my grandfather was her fifth husband. I knew that for some reason her nose looked very different in person than it did in the pictures taken when she was younger. All we had heard of her childhood was that she lived on a Native American reservation in a tent with a dirt floor, and that her brother stopped going to school in junior high because her family could not afford to buy shoes.

Years after my grandmother passed, we were recounting this story to her brother when he said, "None of that ever happened." Shortly afterward, I took a DNA test to find out more about my heritage. When the results came back, they revealed I have no Native American ancestry. When I called my sister to tell her, she happened to be picking her daughter up from school on Heritage Day; my niece had gone dressed in traditional Native American attire.

I am not sure why my grandmother told us those stories about her childhood if they weren't true. I wish I could have learned more about her past. Perhaps it was too painful for her, so she made up stories instead. People keep secrets for all sorts of reasons, but we should have at least some places where those barricades can come down fully—one of them being family. In order to cultivate these environments, we need to keep asking questions with kindness.

Eventually, we can begin to replace the lies with healthy boundaries. If you want people to tell you the truth, they need to know you will still love them after you hear it.

You may currently be navigating a lonely season of life. Perhaps you are physically far away from your family—or perhaps you live next door but have lost emotional connections with them. It is never too late to engage with your family, friends, and neighbors. While relationships are a two-way street and you cannot control how others will respond, you can begin to explore your role in the situation. You may find this challenging, but the freedom that awaits you on the other side of this exploration will be well worth it.

Method Three: Keeping Up with the Joneses

As we grow up, we play the comparison game with our friends and neighbors. You might notice yourself being a little jealous that they could afford that vacation or wishing that you had an impressive car like theirs. Misdirection will have us thinking that keeping up with the Joneses is more important than caring for the Joneses. We can get so focused on advancing our lives that we stop appreciating how great we have it.

I made many friends in magic before I started pursuing it as a career, but something shifted as I grew older. I began to build my business by performing at local parties and events. As my desire for making a name for myself grew, I began to view other performers not as my community but as my competition. Sadly, I missed out on many years of friendship because I lost sight of how important those relationships were. I am happy to say now that some of my best friends are fellow performers. We encourage each other through the ups and downs of this business, and I am so glad that I once again have discovered the value of genuine relationships with them.

My relationship with misdirection began with a trip to the local magic shop when I was seven years old. If you have never been to a brick-and-mortar magic shop, then you haven't felt the rush of being introduced to shelf after shelf of mysterious objects that you won't find anywhere else on earth. The walls are usually lined with antique, built-in wooden shelving. Picture an old-timey hardware store—but here, all the hammers are made of rubber. You can get a box that helps you cut someone in half, a sword that you can shove through someone's neck, poison...(OK, not poison, but seriously—why are so many magic tricks so violent? A Vegas magic show is essentially some guy almost committing murder, but then we find out he didn't commit murder and he is in the audience behind you on a motorcycle.)

It didn't take much for me to get drawn into this world of odd-balls and outcasts. Everyone I met was so nice. They had information I didn't have, and if I was willing to practice and invest a little time and money, they would share the secrets with me. It didn't matter that I was just a kid. Most places in life were reserved for adults, but at the magic shop, anyone was welcome.

One of the first things I bought there was the French arm chopper. As a child, I wasn't sure what made this device French. (Did it only work on people who had stolen baguettes?) I just saw it and had to have it. It was painted electric blue with bright yellow accents. It had a hole in it where you would place the volunteer's hand, and just below that was a basket where the hand would land after the razor-sharp blade came crashing down. They sold me this miniature guillotine when I was just ten years old, and I used it while performing for seven-year-olds.

On Friday nights after the store closed, our local magic club would meet. The elders of the group would perform and then explain one miracle after another. I watched with wide eyes as the godfather of the club, then in his eighties, reached into the air and produced an endless stream of cards from his empty hand before dropping them into his fedora. The method was so diabolical that learning the secret made it even more amazing.

These older magicians were so excited that the next generation was interested in the art, that they gave us opportunities we didn't earn. I still remember when the shop owner, who also produced the weekly Saturday night show, asked if I wanted to perform the sword box illusion that weekend. I said I would love to, but I didn't have the prop, so he let me borrow his—which cost several thousand dollars and was custom-made to do the impossible. This performer invested in me because he saw my potential. He didn't see me as a threat or his competition, just someone he could help. His passion for the magical outweighed any concern he had about me breaking the prop or competing with him.

All of this joy came from developing true community that was devoid of unhealthy competition. We create a lot of misdirection in our own minds as we try to pass each other in the rat race. Instead of falling into this comparison trap, which only steals our joy, what if we decided to be the best at building community?

Method Four: Believing That Real Community Doesn't Exist

It is natural to want to belong, to have a group of people who get you and are glad when you show up. My parents loved the TV show *Cheers* when I was a kid. There was a character named Norm who was hailed as a hero just for walking into the bar every day. I wanted to be Norm.

It is tempting to believe that a real, genuinely supportive community is impossible to find. The truth is, real community can exist wherever you are if you take a genuine interest in others and look for opportunities to engage.

It doesn't take huge gestures to make special moments for the people in your community. As with a great magic trick, sometimes the simplest things have the biggest impact.

I loved Halloween growing up, and now my kids do, too. Over the last few years, we've established a new tradition. After our kids are done trick or treating, they love to come back and pass out candy to others. I set up a Bluetooth speaker in the front yard and connect my phone to Spotify. One of our girls stands on the porch ready to pass out candy while the other waits at the end of the driveway and announces the names of the characters the other children are pretending to be. I will then quickly find a song on Spotify associated with those characters. The look on the kid's faces as their character's theme song blasts through the speakers is priceless. It's a truly magical moment. Recently, one little girl was dressed as Elsa from *Frozen*, and she began to dance with her mom as "Let It Go" began to play. Two kids dressed in *Star Wars* costumes had a lightsaber battle as I played that theme song. Tiny things like this make the neighborhood feel more like a community. If you want to make a big impact in your community, start with small gestures.

An idea attributed to Martin Luther King Jr. is that we all choose whether we will be a thermostat or thermometer in life. Thermometers just report what the temperature is. In your work environments, in your family, if you choose to be a thermometer, you will constantly just be pointing out the problems. But thermostats change the environment. If something feels off or uncomfortable, you can shift the thermostat ever so slightly and the entire room will change to match the temperature it sets. We have this same ability when it comes to our outlook and actions. Instead of simply complaining that things aren't good, we can set a standard of positivity and encouragement that the rest of the room will rise to meet.

One summer our family began a road trip feeling ultra-prepared. We had packed the snacks and planned stops for bathroom breaks. With kids and dogs in tow, we headed out for a perfect eight-hour drive. For the first five hours, it was smooth sailing—and then everything ground to a complete halt. It turned out there was some construction going on nearby and the workers had dumped a pile of building materials all over the two-lane highway.

At some point during the three hours that our highway was turned into a parking lot, I stopped being the fun dad. I was upset, my family was upset, and my bad attitude only made it worse.

Then one of my kids said something that turned it all around: She said it reminded her of the opening scene of the movie *La La Land,* which takes place in the middle of LA rush-hour traffic. No one is moving at all, and people are annoyed, but then it turns into a spontaneous dance party.

Something clicked when she said that. I realized that if I could change my perspective, this setback could be a memorable moment. I stopped thinking about how it was negatively impacting us and realized we were surrounded by a community of strangers who probably all felt the same way we did. So we got out of the car and started asking the people in the other cars if they wanted to help us recreate the opening scene of the movie—and almost all of them said yes. Within a few minutes, we were dancing in the street with our newfound friends, and the entire mood on the highway shifted. Of course, that didn't fix the issue on the road, but it made the moment a lot more bearable.

What if we could return to that sense of childlike wonder and look for ways to make each day better for the people around us? Sometimes we need a moment of silliness to snap us out of discouragement. Everyone walked away that day with a memory I'm sure they will share for years to come because a kid decided to see the world differently than the adults around her. I have watched her develop deep and meaningful relationships by approaching life with this attitude.

Remember also that little shifts make a difference over time. When the environment is harsh, it will take more time to adjust the temperature. However, if we are patient, we will see it is possible to make a lasting difference. Instead of just restating the problems around us, let's see how we can help provide the solution. If you want your neighborhood to be different, start by investing in the lives of your neighbors. When we see people not as competition but as friends with whom we are sharing the road of life, it changes everything. By working together, we can accomplish things that never would have been possible on our own.

QUESTIONS TO CONSIDER REGARDING YOUR FAMILY AND COMMUNITY

1. What masks have I been wearing that are keeping genuine connection at bay?
2. Where can I be my truest self?
3. Does my family know the real me? If the answer is no, why not?

4. Who is in close proximity to me physically but not relationally? Do I really know my neighbors? How can I take my connection with my neighbors to the next level?
5. Have I spent enough time getting to know my physical "neighborhood"?
6. What can I do today to be a thermostat in my environments?
7. Who do I need to connect with to learn from their perspective?
8. Am I still comparing myself to others, or have I grown past that?

BROKEN TOOTHPICK

The first time I experienced this trick, it blew my mind. I say "experienced" because it is more than something you just watch happen: It is very tactile and undeniably impressive. It's also easy to do, and if you find yourself at a fancy restaurant, you will most likely have everything you need to perform it.

The great thing about this trick is that toothpicks are cheap. Magicians who want to make this trick more impressive have figured out ways to "destroy" an item that is one of a kind. Borrowing someone's cell phone, wallet, or watch and demolishing it in front of their eyes is a great setup for an illusion because we all know these things are unique and valuable—just like you, or your child or sibling. Misdirection may do the most damage in the home. Never forget, there is only one you, and you have only one family.

The Trick

The performer shows both sides of a cloth napkin to the spectators before laying it flat on the table. A toothpick is placed in the
center of the napkin, and the four corners are folded in to cover it.
A volunteer is asked to feel the toothpick through the cloth, then
the performer asks him to break it in several places. The volunteer
can feel this happening, and the other spectators can hear the
toothpick breaking. The performer says a few magic words and
then unfolds the napkin to reveal the toothpick—unbroken and
whole. He can even hand it out for examination.

The Secret

To perform this illusion, you will need a cloth napkin and two
wooden toothpicks. Most dinner napkins have a hem sewn around
the outside edge; tuck one of the toothpicks into this hem to make
it invisible to the audience. This toothpick will be destroyed during
the performance.

Hold the napkin up by the corners so your audience can see one
side, then the other, before placing it on the table with the edge
containing the toothpick nearest to you. Place the second toothpick
in the center of the napkin and begin folding in the corners of the
cloth so they go just past the center. Begin with the corner to your
right, then left, followed by the one closest to you (which contains
the toothpick), and finally the one farthest away. It is important to
keep an eye on where you place the edge with the toothpick in it
before you cover it up with the last side of the napkin.

Hold the napkin so that the toothpick hidden in the seam is
held between your fingertips. Allow your volunteer to destroy this

toothpick. These broken pieces will remain there, so there is nothing to hide. Once everyone is satisfied that it is broken, unveil the other toothpick, showing that it is whole.

To see a video breaking down how this trick is performed, visit **taylorhughes.com/misdirection**.

CHAPTER 8

MISDIRECTING OURSELVES

When young magicians start out, they are told to practice in front of a three-angled mirror to see what each trick looks like from several different angles, including the spectators' point of view. This works great, except for the fact that you will often blink right when you are making a secret move! When you want to be successful, sometimes you will unknowingly blink to make the effect look better. The solution to this is to videotape yourself and then watch the footage.

To keep from misdirecting ourselves in life, we all need an unflinchingly honest way of assessing ourselves to see what's really going on.

Method One: Thinking Happiness Is a Destination

When I was a kid, I told my mom the only thing I wanted for Christmas was to go to Disneyland. I had a great childhood, but it was predictable—and predictability is the enemy of whimsy.

Every day I would wake up and put on my school uniform before heading out the door. One morning, I woke up to see that my mother had laid clothes out for me, which was unusual. Not only that, but she had laid out a pair of jeans and a Mickey Mouse sweatshirt. Had she forgotten we had a school dress code? When I went downstairs to tell her about it, she informed me that instead of going to school, we would be going to Disneyland! The joy that filled my soul in that moment has been matched at only a few other points since. I imagined all the fun I was going to have, the memories I would make, and the rides I would go on.

When we arrived, the first ride my older sisters wanted to go on was the Haunted Mansion. I don't enjoy being scared, and the idea of that ride terrified me. There's a graveyard in front of it! I waited for my family while they went on it without me because I was too afraid.

Our second ride was Pirates of the Caribbean. I thought for sure this would be great, but as we got to the front of the line, I could hear screams as the boats disappeared down an ominous tunnel. I walked onto a boat, across the bench seat, and straight out the other side, where I waited while my family took the ride without me. I stood by the attendant, terrified the whole time because no one mentioned the ride was sixteen minutes long. I was certain my family had met their demise.

My poor mom, attempting to make this a good experience for me, thought, *Let's go to the kid rides area. Surely there is a ride there that Taylor will go on.* The first we encountered was Mister Toad's Wild Ride, which starts with you running from the police before ending up in jail, dying, and then going to Hell. This was the only ride I went on that day. After that, I was *done.*

I eventually learned to love all the rides, but that first trip didn't live up to my expectations because I made a mistake that we can all make from time to time: I spent a lot of time dreaming about a place, but when I finally got there, I didn't know how to enjoy myself. Some of us have been misdirected because we have believed the lie that someday, when we reach a certain point, we will be happy. Instead, we need to learn to enjoy the journey along the way.

The challenge with basing your joy on your situation is that situations change. True happiness is a result of gratitude. If you want to feel more joyful, a great step is to practice being grateful in your current circumstance. I have friends who make a practice of having all their kids share one good thing that happened or that made them happy that day at the dinner table each night. You can do this exercise as well. Rather than focusing on what you don't have, ask yourself what made you smile today.

Method Two: Setting Impossible Goals

Every January, it happens: The gyms are crowded with new members ready for a change. Office supply stores are buzzing with people looking to get organized, and yard sales abound as neighbors decide it is out with the old and in with the new. Everyone everywhere is making big plans and swearing that this time, things will be different. After all, it's a new year so it should be a new you, right? Within three weeks, most of those resolutions have already petered out.

One of the ways we misdirect ourselves is by thinking that there are quick fixes to our problems. *Sure, work has been challenging, but if I just attend this conference, it will give me the tools I need.* We listen to podcasts that recommend books to read that push us to follow the next guru because maybe they have it figured out. We are constantly searching for a magic ingredient that does not exist.

Finding yourself making the same goals year after year can be exhausting and disheartening. It is easier to trust a stranger who looks like he has it together than to trust ourselves. We don't believe that we have what it takes to really change, and so we look elsewhere for the perfect life hack.

We all have big plans, resolutions, and dreams we want to see come to pass. What if this time around, we decide to work on those dreams, but without the pressure we tend to put on ourselves? I recently took an afternoon off from a big writing project to recharge with a friend. I discovered that while I thought I needed to push myself more, what I really needed was to step away for a moment so I could see it with fresh eyes. We have been taught to hustle and grind, but we also need to rest and refocus. Be kind to yourself. Aim at being present, not perfect. The work that happens in you is just as important as the work you do for others.

Sometimes I fool myself when it comes to eating. I will convince myself that I am going to get healthy and say no to things that are bad for me—and then I go to Texas.

One of the upsides to traveling is I get to experience all sorts of food, which is a great way to connect with people. When I travel, I usually go to unique hole-in-the-wall places or restaurants we don't have in California. I remember the first time I had Whataburger. To be honest, I was disappointed; I thought it was greasy and not great...but thirty minutes later, I wanted another. Now, whenever I go to Texas, I have to stop by Whataburger.

One day, I was in the Dallas airport, waiting for a flight to Chicago, when I saw those orange and white strips on the side of a restaurant on the way to my terminal. They pulled me in like a tractor beam, and I found myself thinking, *I'll just make the best choice possible.*

I immediately decided I wouldn't be having the chicken sandwich or salad on the menu, but I would still eat healthy. I thought, *I'll get a burger with no cheese, and no fries.* But as I waited in line, I saw a photo of a burger, and the cheese looked so good that I decided I would have cheese on the burger but still no fries. About sixty seconds later I thought, "I'll still be hungry without the fries," so I decided to get double meat. *That's extra protein, and protein is good for you. I will still not get fries.* I proudly gave the cashier my order of a double cheeseburger with no fries. Then she told me it was Whataburger Wednesday—meaning buy one burger, and you get another free. She then asked if I would like my extra double cheeseburger, and I said, yes—yes, I would.

So much for eating healthy that day.

We need to take personal responsibility for the areas where we are misdirecting ourselves.

Method Three: Fundamental Attribution Error
Our ability to excuse our actions also affects the way we view other people. Think about the last time you were in a hurry to get

somewhere and someone cut you off on the freeway. How did that make you feel about the other person? Maybe you said out loud, "What a jerk!" Has this ever happened while you yourself were speeding? If so, you may have been misdirected by fundamental attribution error. This is when you attribute your own behavior to circumstance but the behavior of others to their character. You had a good reason for speeding—perhaps you were late for an important appointment. However, you assume that the other driver cut you off because he is a jerk. Is it possible that his behavior was also circumstantial?

Recently, I had the privilege of performing for a group of inmates at California's San Quentin State Prison. While I was honored by the invitation and hoped I could give these men an opportunity to laugh, I was also a little nervous. We can make all sorts of assumptions about people who are incarcerated—that they are all dangerous criminals who are paying the price for the pain they have inflicted on others. We see pictures of fellow humans in handcuffs with captions that read, "Another lowlife behind bars." What I have experienced on my trips to visit our most forgotten citizens is that we misdirect ourselves when we assume we know someone's character because of the circumstances that person is experiencing.

While protecting society from misdirected individuals who seek to cause harm, we also need to also realize that not everyone currently in prison falls into this category. I have gotten to know many inmates over the last few years, and more often than you might think, their fate is the result of being in the wrong place at the wrong time. Some of the most compassionate, hard-working, educated friends I have are serving sentences for poor choices they made when they were young adults. When we see ourselves as good people who make mistakes but assume other people who've made mistakes are evil, we have made a fundamental attribution error.

The antidote to this, again, is asking questions. *What is the story behind the story? How would I feel if I were in that person's shoes?* Practicing empathy is vital.

Another good practice is listing three great things about the person you're tempted to judge. It will remind you that none of us are just one thing. Choosing to look for the good in someone who might be frustrating you in the moment will allow you to step outside the situation and be more compassionate.

Method Four: Neglecting Ourselves

I am so glad self-care is a normal part of our conversations these days. When I was a kid in the 1980s, there was very little talk about mental health and caring for yourself. The Golden Rule was taught to us early on: Treat others the way you would like to be treated. I took this to mean that we should be kind to other people, but I was not always kind to myself. I would talk about myself in ways that I would never speak about another person, as if I were held to a different set of rules.

I have a very loving family, and my parents always made it clear that they loved us and were proud of us. Where did my negative opinions of myself come from? While many things factor into how we view ourselves, I believe the environments where we spend the most time have the biggest impact. For some, this is the office, for others, it is the gym; but for me growing up, it was church.

I had a lot of great church experiences, but it's also reasonable to question where it may have had a negative impact on my view of myself during my formative years.

My church emphasized living sacrificially—that life is not about you as an individual, but others—and that your responsibility is to focus on them. There is a lot of good in this idea. Caring for others is a noble cause. Realizing that you are a part of a community and that we are all connected is a beautiful thing. The challenge comes when we are so externally focused that we fail to care for ourselves.

I remember sitting crisscross applesauce on the carpet as a young kid while my Sunday school teacher told us that we would be learning about joy and how it differs from happiness. Happiness is based on happenings. When good things happen, we are happy, but when bad things happen, we are sad. She told us we can always have joy even when things are not going well. She even created a little acronym to help us remember our priorities: Jesus, then Others, and then You.

At one point in my life, I was so focused on trying to honor God and sacrifice for the church that I neglected my family, friends, and mental health. As I spent more time in church and got involved in leadership, emphasizing others above myself became overwhelming. When I stopped working for the church, it took a long time to stop feeling bad about trying to build a business around my dream of being a magician. I had been taught to only focus on the vision of the church and not my own hopes and dreams.

Maybe you have found yourself leaving a job that discouraged you so much that you stopped dreaming. I want to encourage you that pursuing your passion is not a selfish thing. If you have something in your heart that is not completely self-centered, there is probably a reason you keep thinking about it. No one else on the planet woke up today thinking about your purpose. The world needs dreamers—people who are willing to build something that doesn't exist yet. Sometimes the best way you can serve others is to focus on yourself for a season. The more you invest in your own personal growth, the more you will have to give.

Method Five: Tying Your Value to Your Performance

The misdirected idea that our value is based on our ability to do good work is ingrained in us as children. *If you are good, Santa will bring you a Christmas present. If you eat all your vegetables, you can have dessert. If you do well in class, the teacher will write your name under the smiley face.* When you win or get all the test answers right, it is easy to feel somehow that you are a better person.

I have always been motivated to work and have always been lucky or foolish enough to have jobs that are related to my passions, which made the work much more than a means to an end. But it is strange when your job is to create content you hope other people enjoy and then place your work into the hands of strangers for approval. Tying your value to your ability to perform is dangerous because at some point your performance abilities will decline—and if that's where you have placed all your value, so will your self-esteem.

I have worked with many individuals who have built successful careers and are now trying to figure out what is next. For many of them, financial security is not the big issue they once thought it would be. They have the resources to start something new; their biggest challenge is leaving the familiar. An often-unseen side effect of being really good at something is not knowing who you are without it.

Sometimes these transitions are choices we make out of a desire for something different, and other times they are forced upon us as we age and our skills are no longer as sharp as they once were. Athletes who were once the star players begin spending more time on the bench. Executives who built companies from the ground up are now being asked to step aside as the next generation carries their dream forward. Parents who raised their children with love and care are realizing for the first time that their role is changing now that the kids have grown. Understand that your value is not determined by your ability to perform for others. It is possible to find beauty in every stage of your journey.

I would encourage you to start seeing your value separately from the job you do for others. You are far greater than the sum of your accomplishments. You are irreplaceable. You are one of a kind.

QUESTIONS TO ASK YOURSELF

1. If I take away what I do, who am I?
2. In what ways have I been neglecting self-care?
3. When was the last time I audited my goals? Am I setting realistic expectations for myself?
4. What is a recent victory I haven't taken time to celebrate?
5. Do I believe happiness is attainable? Why or why not?
6. Have I been making fundamental attribution errors about others? If so, what kind? How can I show others more grace?

THREE-ACES TRICK

This is one of the first card tricks I ever learned, and it is based on disguising one card as another. It is a good reminder that masquerading is one of the greatest tools of misdirection.

The Trick

The magician displays a deck of cards on the table, stacked face down. In her hand, she shows that she has removed three aces—the ace of clubs, the ace of diamonds, and the ace of spades. The audience watches as she places one card in the middle of the pack, one card on top, and one on the bottom. She asks a volunteer to cut the cards, then instructs him to spread the cards face up on the table, revealing that the three aces are now back together in the center of the deck.

The Secret

There are two important keys in this trick: time delay and disguising one item as another. We will discuss those in a moment.

This trick uses a standard deck of cards. While the audience is told that the trick happens with three aces, all four are used. Before you approach your spectator, set up the cards so the deck is face down with the four aces face down in the following order on top: the ace of hearts, the two black aces, and the ace of diamonds.

The ace of hearts will be disguised as the ace of diamonds for the beginning of the trick.

To do this, hold the ace of hearts face up in your hand with the point of the heart pointing straight up. Place the ace of clubs on top of the ace of hearts and fan it to the left at a forty-five-degree angle so that the rounded part of the heart is cut off, making a straight line. If you place the ace of spades on top of these two cards and fan it to the right, you will see that you can make the ace of hearts look like the ace of diamonds. It is also important that you are sure to cover the small heart under the A in the corner. (For a video example of this, visit my website at the link on the next page.)

So now you have three aces in your hand—clubs, spades, and hearts disguised as the ace of diamonds. The real ace of diamonds remains face down on top of the deck. Show the three cards to the audience before turning them face down as you remove the middle card (supposedly the diamonds, but in actuality, the ace of hearts). Place this card in the middle of the pack. (It doesn't matter where, because you won't be trying to find it later.) Now place one of the remaining black aces on the bottom of the deck. The last card will be placed on top of the pack, directly on top of the real ace of diamonds.

At this point, all that is left to do is cut the deck. By doing so, the card on the bottom and the two cards on top will be placed together in the center of the deck.

To add to the mystery, you can use a time delay. Have the volunteer cut the cards, but don't complete the cut right away. Ask if it seems like half of the deck to him. Tell him he is going to perform the magic now. Say whatever you want, but take a little time before you have him complete the cut. Adding this time delay will make the volunteer stop thinking about the fact that the cards on the bottom and top will be put together with a simple cut. Then have him spread the cards face up, and accept the audience's amazement as they see that the three cards are all back together again in the middle of the pack.

To see a video breaking down how this trick is performed, visit **taylorhughes.com/misdirection.**

CHAPTER 9

MISDIRECTION
AND ARTIFICIAL INTELLIGENCE

Much of what we saw on movies and TV in the 1980s was speculating about the future. Would we end up in an intergalactic battle over good and evil, like we saw in *Star Wars*? Perhaps our entire life would be automated and more convenient, like what we saw on *The Jetsons*. My biggest question of all came from what I consider to be the greatest movie franchise of all time, *Back to the Future*. By my calculations, I should have had a hoverboard ten years ago. I am still waiting.

Today we are again on the cusp of incredible breakthroughs in technology. There is both a lot of excitement and trepidation regarding the use of artificial intelligence (AI) in everyday life. As we have seen in all areas of life, manipulation and misdirection abound. I obviously cannot predict the future, although I create the illusion that I can onstage nightly. While most of the chapters have been asking how we got where we are, in this section, we ask where we are going. Asking questions now will help us address big concerns before it's too late.

What Is AI?

AI is using computers and other machinery to simulate human intelligence. Shortly after the first robot was developed in the 1950s, people began to talk about robots taking over society one day. Since our primary goal as humans has always been survival, the conversation surrounding AI today is filled with a mix of emotions. Some claim it will help us thrive. Others fear we are creating Frankenstein-esque monsters that will one day rule over us with literal iron fists.

You've likely encountered AI already without realizing it. For example, while looking for information about an order you placed online, you notice a little flashing light at the side of the page. When you click it, a chat box appears with the words: "Hi, I'm Alex. May I help you?" You might go on to have a perfectly delightful conversation with Alex without ever realizing you are actually conversing with an AI bot that has taken the place of a customer service representative.

Speaking of bots (early AI), you may have seen them in action on social media, ganging up on a tweet the bot's controller doesn't like. Meanwhile, in a New York publishing house, an editor needs a design for a book cover, which she can get in a snap from ChatGPT (without waiting for or paying a copywriter to create one). ChatGPT is an AI chatbot—software.

You've undoubtedly seen ads online for clothing worn by a model created solely by AI—no humans were involved in that particular photo shoot! You also may have seen "photos" on social media depicting aging, overweight politicians as muscular young men in heroic poses. The photos look realistic, and some people find them amusing, but taken a step further—a false black eye, for example—the wrong story can be told. It's easy to see that harm is only a short step away.

Recently, some politicos have taken to creating video "campaign" advertisements with AI—and the only reason you know is because sometimes the images are completely unrelated to the claims being made. (Example: A Russian military plane is said to be an American plane, or an invading army claimed to be China invading Taiwan.) This sort of thing used to be done with Photoshop, but AI is several degrees harder to detect—especially for the uninitiated—and this sets misdirection in motion.

It is important to weigh these positives and negatives and set up structures to support the future we intend to create. We have activated a launch sequence that cannot be reversed, and AI is advancing at an incredible rate. New laws are already being implemented, but big decisions still need to be made. If we don't decide how to limit AI now, we may lose the opportunity to be the ones who call the shots.

What Are the Potential Benefits?

Increased efficiency is almost guaranteed when using AI to complete tasks normally done by humans. Computers can work twenty-four hours a day. They don't need time off to sleep, take a vacation, or have a baby. AI deals only with facts and figures, not emotions. Productivity is increased as you remove the limitations of human labor; you simply work the machine until it runs down. Then you replace it, and you never have to meet with HR. Computers also remove the element of human error. Training AI to catch details that a human can overlook could positively impact product quality and consistency.

Cost savings over time can be a benefit as well. While there is a large upfront investment and a maintenance budget is required, a computer doesn't need raises, benefits, or rewards. You don't have to pay it more for working overtime, and you don't have to worry about it leaving to take a better opportunity. You avoid the risk of paying workers' compensation because it won't get injured on the job, and you reduce employment liabilities at the same time. In fact, you can implement AI in place of humans in risky or dangerous situations.

Decisions are made more quickly when you don't need to take their impact on the workforce or other relational dynamics into account. Problems are solved through the vast reservoir of data the machine has received and stored. Machines don't forget what they have learned or have lapses of judgment. They do what they are programmed to do every time.

New inventions become possible as technology advances rapidly. Computers can be trained to look for ways to improve their own programs. What's more, it means customer support is now available twenty-four seven. AI is trained to address issues and appease customers without the need for a human representation. With all these positives, it is easy to think, *What could possibly go wrong?* Well, many things. Let's take a look.

Misdirection and Other Possible Downsides

Human job loss is almost inevitable once AI comes on the scene. Some may argue that AI will create new jobs in the areas of computer programming, production, and maintenance; however, the number of jobs that will become obsolete far outweighs the number of new opportunities. We aren't far away from being able to take a driverless car to a coffee shop that is completely computerized before buying tickets to a movie without interacting with a single human employee of any of those establishments.

That may sound like an improvement—but if you cannot afford to do any of those things because you lost your job to a robot, misdirection has already occurred. This may seem like a risk for entry-level jobs only—but we are already seeing AI being used to do everything from creating art to assisting in heart surgery.[1] Misdirection comes when we seek the benefits of this technology without considering the inevitable drawbacks.

Creative artists are already feeling the impact as companies turn to AI–generated artwork because it is fast and, in most cases, free. It is important to remember, however, that AI generators are not creating new things out of nothing; they are pulling from actual artists' work to create piecemeal compilations by cobbling elements of different works together. These "new" works then become part of the pot from which everything else is pulled. Artists are already growing uneasy about sharing their work because they don't want it to be stolen by a computer.

This leads us to the topic of ownership and plagiarism. If a computer is prompted to write a script, who owns that work? Not only did the person initiating the project not do any real work, but what he receives will be a compilation of other people's published work—without credit being given to those authors. AI is tailor-made for the theft of intellectual property, and lawsuits over this are already being filed.[2]

One of the issues that led to the 2023 Hollywood writers' strike was their request for more regulations on using AI to create scripts for film and television. The agreements that are already in place refer to writers as people, so technically, AI could not receive writing credit. However, there is concern that at least portions of the work will be taken over by AI. Instead of paying for a team of professional writers, studios could have unpaid interns cranking out scripts based on prompts in a matter of seconds. While this is all being discussed, studios continue to operate and stream under the old rules, bringing in money while the people who brought those shows to life struggle to make ends meet.[3]

Teachers have already seen the negative effects of students using AI to "write" research papers. Bots are now advanced enough to write things with a specific voice and viewpoint, and that will continue to change the way we teach and measure education. One friend of mine who is a teacher has resorted to having her students write every essay in class to keep them from using AI to do their homework.

As human interaction becomes minimal, social dynamics will change as well. Working and interacting with others daily is a big part of how we learn to communicate and care for people. We saw the impact that minimizing interaction had on our communities during the COVID-19 pandemic. Studies show that isolation leads to depression, anxiety, and an increase in family violence.[4] Imagine what might happen if you spent every day without interacting with the strangers who happen to work at your local restaurant, bank, or retail store. Communication and social skills would be impacted, making us less likely to connect with the few humans we regularly interact with.

Of course, most concerning is the idea that someone might weaponize AI to use against humans. Imagine an army of AI soldiers who don't fear death being trained to attack without any concern for human rights. Now what happens if an enemy gains access to these soldiers and reprograms them to attack the citizens of that country? While this sounds like something out of a sci-fi movie, it is within reach. If we can use something for good, manipulators will always find a way to use it for evil. The same can be said of any object. A knife can be used as a tool for good or a weapon for evil. The difference in this case is that knives aren't constantly learning and adapting on their own initiative, but AI is.

We are already seeing AI used to influence people in elections. When Joe Biden announced he would be running for reelection in 2024, the Republican National Committee responded with a commercial using AI-generated images painting a picture of how life might look if that happened. It contained bleak photographic images that had actually been taken during the previous administration, which, of course, is misleading on multiple levels. Similarly, Twitter was buzzing with AI-generated images of former President Donald Trump being arrested that users tried to pass off as real.[5] AI already looks pretty good; eventually, it will be undetectable.

The judicial system as a whole could be thrown into turmoil as it becomes easier to create "evidence" that isn't real. AI is already able to do a pretty good job of creating images using not only your image, but your voice. Videos can be created to make it look as though you are the criminal who stole the item in question, or just as easily show you being in another state when the crime was committed, proving your innocence. Validating evidence will take longer and slow down the judicial process immensely.

What happens if a robot commits a crime? Can humans sue AI? What about robots' rights? A discussion about whether artificially intelligent beings should have rights is already taking place.[6] These are just a few of the questions we aren't yet prepared to answer, and which many haven't even thought to ask yet.

Regulating AI

There are definitely plenty of reasons to push the pause button on AI. At least seventeen states have already introduced legislation on AI, with at least nine already having passed new regulations.[7] However, the domino effect that has been set in place is moving so fast that we may not be able to catch up. What regulations should we implement right away to protect us from being manipulated by the technology we are hoping can support us?

If we look back at the areas of misdirection mentioned throughout this book, we can ask some questions about where we might be heading in each one. When it comes to utilizing AI in marketing and sales, it would be beneficial to require companies to disclose if AI-generated content exists in their ads. While laws concerning truth in advertising already exist, they may need to be rewritten or modified to include the use of AI-generated ads. The same should be true of the media, where the concern over credibility is a thorny issue thanks to a few major publications that have already been busted for using AI to generate articles.[8]

Political campaigns are already making use of this technology. There need to be strong rules in place in order to avoid manipulating people with the use of AI-generated imagery. In June 2023, the staff of Florida Governor Ron DeSantis, who was vying for the Republican presidential nomination, posted an AI-generated image of former President Donald Trump hugging Anthony Fauci with the caption "Real Life Trump," sparking outrage throughout the party, and concern elsewhere.[9]

What happens if your pastor's sermons are not the result of personal study and reflection, but instead are produced in seconds by AI? Why should the church keep people on staff to pass the faith on to the next generation when we can program AI with Scripture and have it teach them instead? Who is going to make those calls?

As with every other type of writing or content generation, AI should be required to use first-person source information in order to avoid diluting the truth with hearsay and to document the source of its information whenever going straight to the horse's mouth is not an option. We should consider safety reviews and test periods, similar to what the FDA does with new drugs, before implementing AI upgrades.

The misinformation we've discussed is just scratching the surface of what may be possible in the future. As we continue to train machines to take our places, some fear that at a certain point they will become independent. What happens when a military drone is able to select its own targets? What if machines trained to operate at the most efficient level begin to believe that humans are the biggest threat to the planet? This may seem like it's been taken straight from the script of *The Terminator*, but we are on track for these hypothetical situations to become real-life possibilities, and we need to be prepared.

Remembering the Human Element

The one thing AI cannot do is create emotional connections. AI isn't great at gauging tone. It will answer questions—but what happens if we ask the wrong questions? The National Eating Disorders Association stopped using a chatbot to provide customer support because it began dispensing dieting advice based on visitors' questions, which can be detrimental to someone struggling with an eating disorder.[10]

Take it a step further: What happens when the person thinks the advice is coming from another human? If you think it's hard explaining to your parents how the television remote works, imagine trying to explain to someone who doesn't understand technology that the news anchor on TV is not a real person, and that even the script of the story was generated by artificial intelligence. We need to remember the human element. Computers can create songs based on music theory and chord structure, but currently can't move you the way human-created art does. The reason incredible athletes impress us is the fact that they are human. We understand the difficulty of what they are doing, recognize that they had to train hard to do it, and appreciate the outcome of their hard work.

We cannot downplay the importance of human connection in our experiences. We have seen this already with fast food. It may be cheaper, available on demand, and inexpensive, but it isn't the same as having a passionate chef create something beautiful for you to enjoy. With AI, we run the risk of turning every kind of life experience into fast food and losing the things that make it special. During the COVID-19 pandemic, we saw what happened when certain jobs were labeled "nonessential." Some industries and individuals are still trying to recover financially and emotionally from that season of realizing life could go on without them. What will happen to our society when AI renders entire industries nonessential?

What kind of world do we want to live in? The future of AI still lies in the hands of humans deciding whether to protect society by limiting AI or using it to misdirect and manipulate others. AI is the new space race, and if we are so focused on being the first to see the future, we may not like what we see when we get there.

QUESTIONS TO CONSIDER REGARDING AI

1. Is this image or video that is raising my blood pressure artificially generated?
2. Why did the creator use AI? Are the artificial images covering up something that is true? Or creating something false to distract from the truth?
3. Should we automate everything we have the ability to automate? Why or why not?
4. How will we protect each other from AI misuse?
5. AI could replace humans in many jobs. How will our society care for those people?
6. What boundaries do I want to put in place for myself when it comes to utilizing AI?

BEHIND THE CURTAIN #9

MY FRIEND THE WIZARD

Here is a simple trick you can do at your next dinner with friends that is sure to amaze.

The Trick

This is a playing card trick that uses no cards at all. As you explain this to your unsuspecting volunteer, you also share that you have a friend who can read minds even if he isn't in the same place as the person whose mind is being read. To prove it, you tell your volunteer to think of any card at all; you will call your friend, and he will tell you which card the volunteer is thinking of. In case the volunteer thinks there is any funny business going on, you can even use his phone to call your mind-reading friend. The volunteer agrees, and you ask which card he has chosen. (Let's say he picks the five of

147

hearts.) You dial your friend's number and then pass the phone to your volunteer. The person on the other end of the line says, "I have a feeling you are thinking of the five of hearts." You will have to catch the phone as the volunteer drops it in shock.

The Secret

The secret to this effect lies in the fact that the person the trick is being performed on only hears one part of your conversation when you dial your "psychic" friend. He hears you say, "May I speak to the wizard?" and then say, "Yes, they are here" before you pass over the phone. This seems innocent because you have not told the mind-reader anything that would let them know what the card is.

But what actually happened is you told your friend you would be calling around this time, so as soon as he gets on the phone, he begins calling out card values slowly. What you hear, as the performer, is the person on the other end saying, "Ace…two…three," etc. As soon as he gets to the value of the card—in this case, five—you say, "May I speak to the wizard?" Your friend now knows the volunteer is thinking of a five. He then begins calling out the suits—clubs, hearts, etc. As soon as he says "hearts," you say, "Yes, they are here." By the time the volunteer gets on the phone, your psychic friend already knows the card he named a moment ago.

To see a video breaking down how this trick is performed, visit **taylorhughes.com/misdirection.**

CHAPTER 10

PICKING UP THE PIECES

This book has focused on spotting and avoiding misdirection. However, there isn't a person walking the planet who has not already experienced some kind of misdirection. What do you do when you are caught off guard by the horrible feeling of knowing that you have been manipulated? How do you trust people going forward? How do you trust yourself and your own decision-making abilities? Let's look at the wake misdirection leaves and how we can learn to rebuild after experiencing it firsthand.

Before we continue, I want to take a moment to mention that I am not a therapist. I am grateful for both the friends and professional counselors who walked with me through a season of rebuilding after I was devastated by misdirection, during which I lost friends and treasured relationships. I highly recommend that anyone looking to work through the trauma of misdirection see a qualified professional therapist. What I share here is not a replacement for the incredible resources mental health professionals can provide, but observations that have helped me in my journey of healing.

Method One: Accepting Reality

Perhaps some of the examples of misdirection I've outlined in this book have felt a little too familiar, as if these are chapters from your own life. Recognizing that you have fallen for misdirection can be a hard pill to swallow. When I found myself blindsided by misdirection, it meant not only the end of a career—I felt like I had lost everything and everyone I had ever known. When misdirection hits home, you can experience a lot of conflicting emotions. Maybe you felt foolish for not seeing the truth earlier, shame for being involved in something that was hurting others, anger over the pain your family experienced, jealous of the people who were able to stay while you had to leave, afraid of the future, or just plain hurt.

It is hard to believe that someone would knowingly take advantage of you. It also can be difficult to admit you have been fooled when you are used to being in control. As a result, you might find yourself either intentionally or unintentionally blocking out the traumatic experience. It is possible that the truth of your experience is too overwhelming to even consider. Remember to be patient with yourself and realize there is no cookie-cutter timeline for overcoming manipulation.

As someone who has spent a lifetime studying deception, I was shocked and embarrassed to see how easily I had been misdirected in a place where I felt safe. One step you can take on the road to healing is to acknowledge the reality of what you have experienced. You have been through some really challenging stuff! It is possible to be so sideswiped by misdirection that you just want to ignore what happened and move on, but the process of healing cannot be rushed. Being misdirected or manipulated can leave you feeling like the rug has been pulled out from under you—leaving you feeling hopeless or lost.

Have you ever gotten turned around while trying to find your way through a large shopping mall? When you recognize you are lost, the first step is to acknowledge that you aren't where you want to be. Eventually, you probably found one of those large kiosks with a map showing you where everything is. To get where you want to go, you need to start by acknowledging where you are. Then you can begin to plan a way to reach your destination. If we want to move past moments of manipulation, we need to acknowledge the effect it has had on us; only then will we know how to move forward.

Method Two: Remember What You Have

Misdirection in a well-choreographed magic show can give us experiences of wonder, joy, and elation. Outside the theatrical context, however, misdirection always takes something from us in the form of trust. But in the wake of that wreckage, it can be helpful to realize that all is not lost.

Remember the good people you do have in your life. This may be family, friends, a neighbor, coworker, or therapist. Knowing you have at least one other person who understands and will be there for you goes a long way. One of the side effects of being manipulated is embarrassment. It can be tempting not to share what happened for fear of what others might think. This leads to isolation, but we are not meant to go through life alone. Remember the people who are in your corner and take a moment to be grateful for them. You may even want to keep a journal and take literal notes of the people and things you are grateful for. Simple exercises like this can allow you to see past your current moment.

This brings me to another helpful key: Remembering this moment is just that—a moment, not a permanent state. Your life has not always felt the way it does right now, and it will not always feel this way in the future. Thinking back to days when your current challenges were not the biggest thing in your life can remind you that life is seasonal and that you will find hope again. Make a list of things you love—music, hiking, playing with the dog, whatever lights you up—and keep it close by. When you begin to feel overwhelmed or stuck in a moment of sorrow, choose an activity from the list and make yourself do it.

Another tool you may find helpful is disrupting your day. When we feel stuck, we can feel like we are just getting through life but not living it. Choosing to interrupt this pattern is great for many reasons. One is that it breaks up the monotony and reminds you that you can experience new things. If you tend to walk the same path every day, turn down a different street. If you tend to take warm showers, adjust the temperature to cold. New experiences, no matter how small, can help you believe your future can be different.

Lastly, allow yourself the freedom to have fun. It is possible to experience joy and sorrow simultaneously. If you need to grieve, by all means grieve, but you can still find moments of joy in seasons of sadness. Taking the pressure off and allowing yourself to feel more than one emotion at once is a great gift you can give yourself.

Method Three: Learning to Trust Again

When the misdirection we experience comes at the hands of other people, it can be hard to trust again. Perhaps you have experienced a particularly devastating time when you felt betrayed, abused, or abandoned by people you once considered to be close friends. Our natural reaction to this kind of pain is to close ourselves off from others, to retreat like a turtle into its shell. If you touch the stove and get burned, you are going to be more cautious around it in the future. In order to protect yourself from getting hurt again in relationships, you might commit to not allowing anyone to get close enough to impact you negatively.

It took me a lot of time and therapy to let my guard down after I was hurt. There was a time when I honestly felt like I could never experience friendships as close as the ones I had lost. However, today I am happy to say that the friendships I have developed since that time are deep and rich. It is possible to experience genuine community again. It begins with reminding yourself that it is still available to you.

When you have been the victim of manipulation you find yourself so guarded that you think everyone is out to misdirect you. Looking at everyone with suspicion will rob you of the joy of living today. While it is not possible to completely avoid misdirection, we can learn to recognize it more easily. A good practice while keeping your eyes open for misdirection can be to purposefully look for the good in people and train your mind to notice the wonderful, positive things you find.

Another byproduct of being misdirected is finding it difficult to trust yourself again. After all, if you fell for it before, who's to say it won't happen again? Try paying attention to how certain situations and circumstances make you feel. Have confidence in yourself and what you are experiencing. Ask questions like, "Am I genuinely uncomfortable, or is this just a familiar feeling from a previous misdirected situation?" Encourage yourself and speak kindly to yourself. Overcoming manipulation is a process, and we need to be gentle with ourselves as we go through it. Remind yourself that you are learning and becoming increasingly aware. You are in training.

Method Four: Drawing New Boundaries

Sometimes misdirection is a result of a boundary in our lives being crossed without our permission. Other times it reveals an area where we should have had a boundary but didn't. How many times have you seen a neighbor putting up cameras after something was stolen? He didn't think he needed a security system until it was too late. Perhaps you didn't have safeguards in place to protect you because you couldn't imagine that you would ever end up as you have.

What types of boundaries do you need to put in place to keep from being misdirected again? These will vary based on the circumstances, but an easy way to find your boundaries is to look at where things went wrong. It would be like having critters in your attic: Your first question would be to find out where they are getting in and block that path. Take a moment right now to think about your situation. Is there a moment when you could have avoided misdirection before it showed up? If so, what can you do to prevent it from happening again?

If we do not establish boundaries in our lives, the people and circumstances around us will make decisions for us. If you don't make a point of being home from work by a certain time, the demands of the job will keep you at the office later than you want to be. Anticipating situations in which you may find yourself and setting boundaries now will support you in the long run.

Method Five: Forgive? Forget?

Can I be honest? I like to hold grudges. I know that isn't good. It actually does more harm to you than the person you're refusing to forgive. I get all that, but I also know what it feels like to see the very people who abused you continue on with their lives after trying to destroy yours. For many years I would go to sleep at night thinking, *Maybe tomorrow, justice will come.* While I still wouldn't throw a party to celebrate the people who hurt me, I can say with all sincerity that those feelings of wishing they would get a taste of their own medicine have faded further and further into the background. In fact, I rarely think of them at all.

A turning point was when I realized that the people who misdirected me were victims of misdirection as well—that whether they realized it or not, they were suffering from their own inauthenticity. And I realized that for many years, I lived under a similar illusion. I am so grateful that I have been set free from my old way of being. How could I *not* hope that everyone—including those who wished me harm—would find that same freedom?

This doesn't mean I have forgotten what happened or that I am ignorant enough to think I am the last to suffer because of the choices those people made. I have strong boundaries in place now and will do everything I can to protect others, but I also realize that when you choose to not waste energy in anger, you take away the power those people had over you. I don't know if "forgiveness" is the right word. Some of the people you wish weren't in your life may still be there only because you are hanging onto them in your mind. With that, I guess the word I'm leaning into is "release."

Method Six: Believing the Best

Misdirection can leave us feeling hopeless. It is easy to think it will happen to us again and we won't be able to find real community. We say things like, "Forget it, this is too hard, everyone is bad, and I don't want or need anyone else. I can live life by myself in my own shell." Not only does this rob you of relationships with other wonderful—yes, flawed, but amazing—people, but it robs others of the gift of you. We all need each other. Becoming cynical and assuming the worst of people is not going to help you develop deep and meaningful relationships.

When determining whom to allow into your life—and how far—always remember why you are asking the questions you are asking. You are not trying to catch someone messing up, and you aren't only looking out for yourself. The reason we ask these questions is to protect ourselves and others from manipulation. We want to create a world in which people protect and care for each other. We want to seek truth and create safe environments for future generations to thrive. We want people to be themselves and not feel like they need to put on a show for others. We want leaders to have integrity and empower the people they serve. Here are some questions that will help ensure we stay true to who we want to be.

QUESTIONS TO CONSIDER WHEN PICKING UP THE PIECES

1. Where did things go wrong?
2. Who do I need to release from my life?
3. Who can I lean on during this time?
4. What activities bring me joy?
5. What am I thankful for today?
6. What boundaries can I put in place to safeguard myself in the future?

ONE-AHEAD PRINCIPLE

Magicians often use this principle to fool us because they are one step ahead of their audience when they perform their tricks. Here is an example of how we can beat misdirection at its own game by asking questions and staying one step ahead of it.

The Trick

The performer brings out a pad of paper and claims he will be able to predict the choices the volunteer will make. A volunteer is chosen and asked to clear her mind. The performer asks her to simply think of the name of her childhood pet, and writes something down before crumpling the sheet of paper and setting it on the table.

"What was the name of your childhood pet?" he asks.

The volunteer responds that she had a cat named Tabby. The performer smiles and says, "Great. Now I want you to think of your favorite two-digit number." Again, he writes down his best guess, crumples the paper up, and sets it next to the other wad of paper on the table.

Then he asks the volunteer to name the number she was thinking of, and she says, "Twenty-seven." The performer smiles again, as if he knew it the whole time.

The magician asks to try one more experiment: This time, he will write down the name of a playing card. He does so, crumples up the paper, and sets it on the table with the other two wads. Then he takes out a deck of cards and asks the volunteer to choose one and hold that image in her mind. (Let's say that in this case, the volunteer selected the four of clubs.) Our performer grabs the three wads of paper on the table, opening them one at a time to show that they read "Tabby," "twenty-seven," and "the four of clubs." The audience erupts into applause.

The Secret

To perform this trick, you will need three sheets of paper, a pen, and a deck of cards. (Be ready to force a card as we described earlier.) Before you approach your volunteer, decide what your force card will be; this is the first thing you will write down.

The first question you ask is the name of the volunteer's childhood pet. There is no way you could know this without some deep Facebook research. However, you don't need to do this, because as you ask them to think of the name, you write down and crumple up the sheet of paper with the name of the card you will force at the end. When the volunteer answers, smile as if that is what you just wrote down.

Next, ask the volunteer to name their favorite number. Before she answers, you write down the name of the pet she just mentioned, crumple up the paper, and set it to the left of the first wad of paper on the table. When the volunteer tells you her favorite number, act pleased and tell her that now you are going to write down the name of a card. Of course, you actually write down the number the volunteer just named. Crumple the sheet of paper and set it on the table between the other two wads. This way, when you read them from right to left, they will be in the correct order.

To see a video breaking down how this trick is performed, visit **taylorhughes.com/misdirection**.

COMMITTING TO CHANGE

I remember the moment when my fourth-grade teacher told us that every day, we would have twenty minutes of reading time. We could choose any book from the library to read at our desks. At first, I was disappointed because most of the books were on subjects in which I had no interest, but then I saw it—*Spooky Magic*. This was a book that not only taught magic tricks, but also pranks you could do on your friends. It was as if the author had created this piece of literature just for me. My favorite prank was cutting a small hole in a cardboard box so you could place your finger inside while holding it; with the addition of a little ketchup, you could make it look like you had a severed finger. I remember showing this to my family members and thinking I was a comedic genius.

Spooky Magic was the most taboo material I could imagine finding at my Christian elementary school. How it got past the librarian's critical eye, I will never know, but I devoured it. I spent the whole reading time that first day studying the first trick before carefully hiding the book in a part of the shelf where I thought no one else would look for it, planning to retrieve it the next day and study some more. I repeated this process for a whole week before someone found my hiding spot and took the book before I could! I watched, horrified, as he flipped through the book, learning the secrets I had sworn to protect. I watched where the other kid placed it—and that day, I stole the book and never returned it! I was a straitlaced kid, but I had to protect the magic secrets.

I had nearly forgotten about this brief brush with criminal behavior until recently, when I was cleaning the attic and found that copy of *Spooky Magic*. A rush of nostalgia hit me as I flipped through the pages, seeing the familiar illustrations and explanations that shaped so much of my childhood. But I also felt a wave of sadness—because to keep secrets, I had done something I shouldn't have.

This is important. If we are going to fight misdirection, we need to own up to the fact that at times, we have been part of the problem. At times we can all get a little sidetracked from what is truly important—but it is never too late to change. If we want the world around us to be different, we can start by making healthy changes personally. We only get to control ourselves, but remember that as you move away from the things that have been misdirecting you, the ripple effects will impact those around you.

Returning to Awe

The thing that first drew me to magic was the overwhelming curiosity of not knowing how things were being done. As we go through life, we collect information about everything we see, ask questions, and study until we feel like we have mastered a topic. If you have ever watched a child trying to tie his shoes for the first time, you know the spectrum of emotions he experiences as he goes from thinking he will never be able to do it to handling it like a pro. When you put on your shoes today, you probably didn't think about tying the laces at all. This is because you have placed "tying my shoes" in the knowledge category. You know how to tie your shoes, so you have decided you don't need to examine that topic anymore. Things become second nature, and we only revisit them when we need to explain them to someone else.

The challenge comes when we think of ourselves as experts in areas of life where we are meant to remain learners. When we think we have it all figured out in marriage, we are in trouble. Businesses that were once considered leaders in their fields are left in the dust when those who run them begin to think they have nothing left to learn or improve. As a magician, my favorite thing is watching people's reactions to tricks, not because I fooled them, but because that is when they realize they were fooled already by thinking they had the trick all figured out.

For too much of my life, I prided myself on how much I knew. It felt good not only to have confidence in my knowledge of how the world worked, but also to be a resource for other people trying to figure it out. Not only did I feel like I was on the right track, but I also made a living by guiding others who wanted to find the right

MISDIRECTION

path for their lives. I wish I had realized earlier that we are all fellow learners, navigating the ups and downs of life together. I missed out on seeing other perspectives because I had misdirected myself into believing that my viewpoint was the best. Most of us already have some idea where we might be off track; we don't need people to point fingers at us, but we do need people who can remind us who we want to be.

In school, we are rewarded for completing education in different subjects. We love checking boxes and feeling like we have put in the time to master that field of knowledge. But if we start thinking we have nothing else to learn, then we are already being misdirected. However, when we position ourselves as learners, possibilities open up and wonderful adventures await. Let's never lose our sense of wonder. There are new thoughts to discover, places to explore, and friends to make.

Every great discovery that changed the world throughout history came from a position of curiosity and wonder. Allow those things to become a daily practice in your life. You may want to find one part of your day in which you have no other obligations but to just sit and ask questions. For me, this is best early in the morning or late at night—a time when work and family are taken care of, when I will not be interrupted by anything other than my own thoughts.

Give yourself the space to reexamine old ideas and introduce new ones. Read a book by someone whose experience is different from your own. Immerse yourself in someone else's world. Hearing their opinion or experience may not mean you will change your mind—in some cases, you may walk away more confident in the beliefs you already hold. But sometimes, you might encounter a new way of thinking that will help you become who you want to be. By allowing yourself to hear other opinions without feeling the need to insert your own, you are setting yourself up for a great adventure. Being open to seeing the world through other people's perspectives will also make us better friends and neighbors.

As you begin to imagine a better future for yourself and those you love, there will be times you need to ask some big questions about the way things are and the way they could be. It is OK to not have life all figured out. Keep pursuing, be kind to yourself and others, and be open to discovery. You never know where you might stumble across the answers you are looking for; they could be right around the corner.

A hundred years from now, there will be all new people. What remains for them will to some extent be the result of what we allow to happen now. If we keep our focus on caring for each other and the world we share, great things are in store for future generations. It starts by asking questions and welcoming back that childhood wonder we once had. Do you remember that feeling from when you were a kid?

I can still smell the way my parents' living room carpet would take on a different aroma as the sun peeked through the curtains on Saturday morning. The rest of the family was still tucked in bed as I lay on the floor, anticipating my favorite moment of the week: Saturday morning cartoons. It being nineteen eighty-something, the closest thing we had to on-demand entertainment was popping a tape into the VCR and watching something we pre-recorded or cracking open a clamshell case that held one of the few made-for-home VHS cassettes we owned. This meant that you had to set appointments so you wouldn't miss your favorite shows.

To this day, early mornings at home are still a sacred time to sit with a cup of coffee or take a walk around the living room to clear my head before my family and I start the day together. However, none of these modern activities hold a candle to the ritual I held when it came to watching my favorite animated shows each weekend. My favorite of all had to be *Scooby-Doo*. I have always been a dog lover, but this dog was the coolest of them all. He loved sandwiches, just like me! He loved adventures, and he and his friends even drove around in a van called "the Mystery Machine." Every episode began the same way: Scooby and his pals would take a wrong turn and end up in a scenario that felt a bit off. Something was wrong, but they couldn't quite tell what it was. Then they would begin asking questions.

While most of the episodes were written to make us think there was some supernatural spook at play, the real culprit was always a sketchy guy with a disguise and ulterior motives. Whoever the villain of the week was would say the same line when their plans got foiled. "I would have gotten away with it, if it weren't for you meddling kids!" This group of friends didn't take things at face value—they asked big questions, and because of that, no one could take advantage of them. If we want to protect the next generation from misdirection, we need to stop raising good boys and girls who just do what they are told.

It's time to raise some meddling kids.

ACKNOWLEDGMENTS

I am so grateful to my family, friends, and neighbors. Our countless conversations about what really matters have been oxygen to my soul. If you found anything of value in this work, it was the result of these people (and many others too numerous to name) who gathered around the family dinner table, evening campfires, hangouts, and late-night trips to the diner.

Katie Hughes, you are the love of my life. We have lived several versions of this life together so far, and each has been more exciting by your side. Thank you for curating a home full of love that allows new friends to feel like family and where family never wants to leave. I can't wait to grow old with you.

To my daughters, Madelyn and Kennedy. Being your dad is the greatest honor I can imagine. Maddy, thank you for taking countless breaks with me to just go for a drive and sing at the top of our lungs. Kennedy, thank you for brainstorming with me about these huge issues in which you are wise beyond your years. You both have shown me how to love people better. Thank you for being my teachers.

To my dear friend, Kim Garcia. Thank you and Tim for being the biggest cheerleaders of the craziest ideas. You have talked me off of some ledges and pushed me off of others. Looking forward to the next adventure.

To my mom and dad, thank you for being unreasonably supportive of everything I have ever done. Thank you to my stepparents and in-laws for breaking every stereotype and being the best.

To all my siblings by birth and by marriage, thank you for being friends by choice.

To Bob and Maria Goff. You have changed our lives in so many ways. Thank you for being a tether of hope when we needed a lifeline. You have been mentors, friends, and coconspirators through the good times and bad.

Thank you to Mary Demuth for your support as I navigated the many versions of this project.

To Jamie Chavez, you have once again helped me find the right words to share these truths.

Kim Stuart, you, my friend, have been a kind and encouraging guide in this world of book writing. I hope to one day be as funny as you.

Thank you, Megan Tibbitts, Jay Desai, and Stephanie Wesson for being the best bunkmates and road companions, on and off the bus.

Adam, Holly, Stefanie, and Justin. I cherish our times under the Oaks.

Thank you to Jack Goldfinger, Richard Barrett, Robert Hall, Vanessa Ragland, and Jamie Flam for providing me with amazing theaters that have become playgrounds.

I am so grateful for friends that have become family: Keith and Melissa Coast, Vance and Chelsea Fite, Mark and Kelly Forster, Eddie Furth, Zac Gandara, Micah and Sabrina Hanson, James Holguin, Mark and Sarah James, Mark and Jinger Kalin, Steve Lopez, Chipper and Lisa Lowell, Matt and Tiffany Marcy, Nick and Kristen Paul, Chris Ruggiero, Dan and Katie Snyder, Rudy and Courtney Zuniga, and Cameron Zvara.

Finally, thank you for reading this book. I hope that by doing so, you experience less misdirection and more magic.

Keep Chasing Wonder,
Taylor

Notes

Chapter 2: Misdirection in the News

1. Jon Simpson, "Finding Brand Success in the Digital World," *Forbes*, August 25, 2017, https://www.forbes.com/sites/forbesagencycouncil/2017/08/25/finding-brand-success-in-the-digital-world/?sh=6d5807e2626e.

2. "Hours of Video Uploaded to YouTube Every Minute as of February 2022," Statistica, June 2022, https://www.statista.com/statistics/259477/hours-of-video-uploaded-to-youtube-every-minute.

Chapter 3: Misdirection in Social Media

1. Nicholas Jackson and Alexis C. Madrigal, "The Rise and Fall of MySpace," *The Atlantic*, January 12, 2011, https://www.theatlantic.com/technology/archive/2011/01/the-rise-and-fall-of-myspace/69444.

2. Craig Silverman and Jeff Kao, "Infamous Russian Troll Farm Seems to Be Source of Anti-Ukraine Propaganda," ProPublica, March 11, 2022, https://www.propublica.org/article/infamous-russian-troll-farm-appears-to-be-source-of-anti-ukraine-propaganda.

3. *United States v. Internet Research Agency LLC*, No. 1:18-CR-00032-DLF (Indictment, February 16, 2018), https://www.justice.gov/file/1035477/download; "Removing Bad Actors on Facebook," Meta, July 31, 2018, https://about.fb.com/news/2018/07/removing-bad-actors-on-facebook.

Chapter 6: Misdirection in the Church

1. Todd M. Johnson, "Christianity Is Fragmented—Why?," Gordon Conwell Theological Seminary, November 6, 2019, https://www .gordonconwell.edu/blog/christianity-is-fragmented-why.

2. "How Much Would It Cost to End World Hunger?," World Food Program USA, August 10, 2022, https://www.wfpusa.org/articles /how-much-would-it-cost-to-end-world-hunger; David P. King et al., "The National Study of Congregations' Economic Practices," Lake Institute on Faith and Giving, https://www.nscep.org/finding.

Chapter 9: Misdirection and Artificial Intelligence

1. "AI Enabled Heart Surgery, Really?," The Keyhole Heart Clinic, March 10, 2019, https://www.thekeyholeheartclinic.com/blog/ artificial-intelligence-enabled-heart-surgery-really.

2. Matt O'Brien, "Sarah Silverman and Novelists Sue ChatGPT-Maker OpenAI for Ingesting Their Books," Associated Press, July 12, 2023, https://apnews.com/article/sarah-silverman-suing-chatgpt-openai-ai -8927025139a8151e26053249d1aeec20.

3. Mandalit del Barco, "Striking Hollywood Scribes Ponder AI in the Writer's Room," NPR, May 18, 2023, https://www.npr.org/2023/05 /18/1176876301/striking-hollywood-writers-contemplate-ai.

4. Pouya Hosseinzadeh et al., "Social Consequences of the COVID-19 Pandemic: A Systematic Review," *Investigación y Educatión en Enfermeria* 40, no. 1 (January–April 2022), https://www.ncbi.nlm .nih.gov/pmc/articles/PMC9052715.

5. Naz Gocek, "Deepfakes versus Democracy," Rewired, https:// stanfordrewired.com/post/deepfakes-democracy; Sophia Cai, "How AI Is Already Changing the 2024 Election," Axios, April 29, 2023, https://www.axios.com/2023/04/29/how-ai-already- changing-2024-election; Rick Hasen, "A Campaign Aide Didn't Write That Email. A.I. Did," *New York Times*, March 28, 2023,

https://www.nytimes.com/2023/03/28/us/politics/artificial-intelligence-2024-campaigns.html.

6. Jessica Peng, "How Human Is AI and Should AI Be Granted Rights?," Columbia Computer Science, December 4, 2018, https://blogs.cuit.columbia.edu/jp3864/2018/12/04/how-human-is-ai-and-should-ai-be-granted-rights.

7. "Legislation Related to Artificial Intelligence," National Conference of State Legislatures, updated August 26, 2022, https://www.ncsl.org/technology-and-communication/legislation-related-to-artificial-intelligence; "US State-by-State AI Legislation Snapshot," Bryan Cave Leighton Paisner LLP, April 13, 2023, https://www.bclplaw.com/en-US/events-insights-news/2023-state-by-state-artificial-intelligence-legislation-snapshot.html.

8. Ian Tucker, "AI Journalism Is Getting Harder to Tell from the Old-Fashioned, Human-Generated Kind," *The Guardian*, April 30, 2023, https://www.theguardian.com/commentisfree/2023/apr/30/ai-journalism-is-getting-harder-to-tell-from-the-old-fashioned-human-generated-kind.

9. Shannon Bond, "DeSantis Campaign Shares Apparent AI-Generated Fake Images of Trump and Fauci," NPR, June 8, 2023, https://www.npr.org/2023/06/08/1181097435/desantis-campaign-shares-apparent-ai-generated-fake-images-of-trump-and-fauci.

10. Staff Writer, "NEDA Suspends AI Chatbot for Giving Harmful Eating Disorder Advice," Psychiatrist.com, June 5, 2023, https://www.psychiatrist.com/news/neda-suspends-ai-chatbot-for-giving-harmful-eating-disorder-advice.

Printed in the USA
CPSIA information can be obtained
at www.ICGtesting.com
CBHW060233020224
3965CB00002B/2